LoRA AND IoT NETWORKS FOR APPLICATIONS IN INDUSTRY 4.0

COMPUTER SCIENCE, TECHNOLOGY AND APPLICATIONS

Additional books and e-books in this series can be found
on Nova's website under the Series tab.

COMPUTER SCIENCE, TECHNOLOGY AND APPLICATIONS

LoRA and IoT Networks for Applications in Industry 4.0

ANITA GEHLOT

RAJESH SINGH

RAVINDRA KUMAR SHARMA

AND

KAMAL KUMAR SHARMA

EDITORS

nova
science publishers
New York

NOTICE TO THE READER

Library of Congress Cataloging-in-Publication Data

ISBN: 978-1-53617-164-8

Published by Nova Science Publishers, Inc. † *New York*

CONTENTS

PREFACE

The concept of Industry 4.0 includes both Internet of Things (IoT) structure and the local networks which need to carry the real-time tasks. The LoRa technology can be implemented for industrial wireless networks to control sensors and actuators of the Industry 4.0 era.

This book aims for exploring the methods and systems to implement LoRa network for industry 4.0.

The book comprises of ten chapters. Chapter 1explains the monitoring of pipeline leaks which plays a prominent role in crude oil industry. To achieve the best solution and more protection of the environment, possible combinations of various technologies are discussed. Chapter 2 illustrates the low power wide area networks. A survey of recent published articleshas been included on Low Power Wide Area networks and their applications. Chapter 3 discusses about the Industrial hazards.It explores the various technical algorithms comprising of various equipments able to monitor environmental parameters by sensing through different pre-installed nodes deployed at specific positions. Chapter 4 deals with smart agriculture with an emphasis on guaranteed nourishment, effects of environmental changes on agribusiness along with lighting and smart parking issues.Chapter 5 proposed a XBEee and IoT based architecture for the monitoring the garbage bins wirelessly. Here the XBee based sensor which is placed in the garbage bin initiates the function of our architecture and sends the status of the garbage bin to the local sever.

Chapter 6 identifies various areas where fire safety technology upgradation is required. The importance of wireless sensor networks as the one of the efficient methods for fire safety systems is also highlighted. Chapter 7 reports a review of research work related to the RSSI. RSSI is concluded as a very good indoor localization approach. Chapter 8 explores the problem of measuring the depth and flow of water in large water body or water pipe. A solution is proposed which will reduce the chance of human error and make pace for intelligent cities. Chapter 9 discusses about the cyber security in manufacturing and related industries. It explores the nature of the data, topologies of IoT devices, and complexities of threat management and ensuring compliance. Chapter 10 addresses the importance of fire safety in smart city and building along with the role of IoT for meeting the requirement.

Editors are thankful to all the contributors and publisher for their support.

Dr. Anita Gehlot
Dr. Rajesh Singh
Ravindra Sharma
Dr. Kamal Kumar

In: LoRA and IoT Networks …   ISBN: 978-1-53617-164-8
Editors: A. Gehlot, R. Singh et al.   © 2020 Nova Science Publishers, Inc.

Chapter 1

ANALYSIS AND DESIGN OF OIL PIPELINE LEAKS MONITORING SYSTEM USING LORA AND IOT NETWORK

Chavala Lakshmi Narayana[1,], Rajesh Singh[2,†], and Anita Gehlot[3,‡]*

[1]ECE, Lovely Professional University, Jalandhar, Punjab, India
[2]SEEE, Lovely Professional University, Jalandhar, Punjab, India

ABSTRACT

Pipelines are more suitable for transporting crude oil from one place to another over a long distance. The monitoring of pipeline leaks plays a prominent role in the crude oil industry. Pipeline leaks happen due to various reasons like illegal tapping, pipe resistance, and third party damages, etc. As pipeline leakage detection systems become more widely deployed in the oil industry, the on-demand for performance dramatically increased. This paper elaborates on the leak detection technologies and

[*] Corresponding Author's Email: Laxminarayana0706@gmail.com.; Chavala Lakshmi Narayana, Research Scholar.
[†] Corresponding Author's Email: srajssssece@gmail.com.; Rajesh Singh, Professor.
[‡] Corresponding Author's Email: dranitagehlot@gmail.com.; Anita Gehlot, Associate Professor.

their usage. To achieve the best solution and more protective of the environment, possible combinations of various technologies are discussed. A proposed system for pipeline leakage monitoring systems using LoRa and IoT technology is presented.

Keywords: Pipeline, Leakage, Tapping, LoRa, IoT, Detection

1. INTRODUCTION

In the Oil industry upstream, middle stream and downstream are the three sectors that play a prominent role in digging oil from wells and supply to consumers. The middle stream plays a major role in the transportation of petroleum products to consumers. Oil pipelines are considered as an economical and safe mode to transport petroleum products over long distances. However, they are subject to hazardous damages like fire, explosions, casualties, and environmental damage that leads to huge economic losses that have severe consequences on human lives and infrastructure [1]. Pipelines that are laid long distances are suffering from natural, operational and mechanical hazards. Pipeline infrastructure damages due to corrosion and third party damages also give that accidental damage of the oil pipelines, like natural disasters, soil movement (e.g., Destroy of foundation, floods, mudslides) and human error [2].

2. REVIEW OF LITERATURE

In this paper, significant onshore pipeline incidents (only refined and crude oil, for petroleum and liquid products are involved and for the gas transmission line is involved) are analyzed and filtered for the actual database to know the frequency of failures. The following conditions are included for incidents.

➢ In-patient hospitalization or fatality and Injury requiring.

> ➢ Out of total cost $50,000 or more, measured in 1984 dollars.
> ➢ Liquid leakage resulting in a fire explosion.

Statistical failure results in various countries like PHMSA in the United States [3], EGIG in Europe [4], UKOPA in the United States [5], and PNGPC in China various countries pipeline issues and frequency of failures were analyzed by comparison. From the year 2004 to 2015 oil pipeline failure frequencies in the US are shown in Figure 1.

Based on the statistical results, the pipeline failures for oil transportation is 432. All of which are happening as significant incidents from the year 2010 to 2015 in the database, the main oil pipeline failure causes are failure of pipe welding material, equipment failure and corrosion shown in figure 2.

During 2004 to 2015, there is no significant variation in property loss and numbers of casualties caused in the US by pipeline accidents, except the value in year 2010 shown in figure 3 which is because of the breaks fire of the Pacific Gas and pipeline of Electric Company's and rupture leakage crude oil by pipeline.

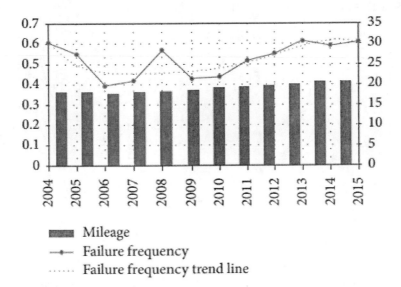

Figure1. Failure and Mileage frequencies for oil Pipelines [3].

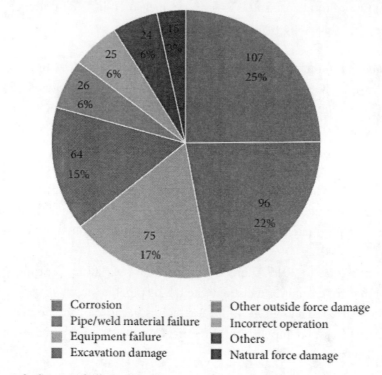

■ Corrosion	■ Other outside force damage
■ Pipe/weld material failure	■ Incorrect operation
■ Equipment failure	■ Others
■ Excavation damage	■ Natural force damage

Figure 2. Causes of oil pipeline [3].

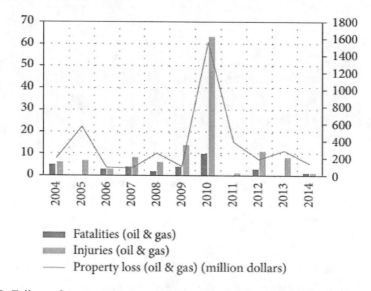

■ Fatalities (oil & gas)	
■ Injuries (oil & gas)	
— Property loss (oil & gas) (million dollars)	

Figure 3. Failure of consequences reported by PHMSA in the US [3].

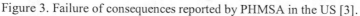

Failure due to Corrosion: For oil pipelines, one of the important factors for pipeline failure is corrosion, and for gas pipelines, corrosion placed third position of all failure factors.

Among those, internal corrosion is mainly of microbiological corrosion.

Due to galvanic corrosion, 60% of external corrosion of pipelines is accounted for.

Failure due to Natural Force Damage: In this aspect, heavy flood/rain and earth movement are the main reasons.

Table 1. Causes and Sub causes from PHMSA [3]

S. No.	Causes	Sub causes
1	*Corrosion*	
	External Corrosion	Acid Water, Corrosive Commodity etc.
	Internal Corrosion and	Galvanic Corrosion,Stray Corrosion etc.
2	*Weld/pipe Material Failure*	
	Fabrication, Construction, and Installation related	Mechanical Damage, Weld Quality in the Field, etc..
	Environmental Related	Deformation Related Cracking, Stress Corrosion Cracking, etc.
	Manufacturing Related	Manufacturing Defect, Weld Quality, etc.
3	*Excavation Damage*	
	Operator's Contractor	Practices locating are not Sufficient, Sufficient excavation for practices.
	Third-Party Damages	One call Notification not Sufficient for practices, Practices locating are not Sufficient and excavation practices are not sufficient.
	Previous Damage due to Excavation Activity	Previous Damage, One-call Notification Practices not Sufficient
4	*Damage due to Natural Force*	Temperature, Earthquakes, Floods/ Heavy Rains.
5	*Wrong Operation*	Damage by Operator's Contractor or Operator, Equipment, No proper installation of Equipment and Overpressure,
6	*Other Damages*	Fire/Explosion and vehicles.

The main causes and sub causes are categorized by PHMSA as in table 1.

Failures due to Failure of Weld Material: While analyzing failure incidents for gas and oil pipelines together, weld/pipe material failure is one of the topmost factors. For sub causes that are analyzed, construction related (backfill dent, field welded girth weld, etc.) accounts 50% and above.

Excavation Failure: In oil and pipeline failure cases, excavation damage is one of the causes in the US, where 15% of oil pipeline failures are accounted for. More percentage of third party excavation damage is accounted for because of insufficient excavation practices and excavation call system.

2.1. Leaks Detection Techniques [1]

In recent years, the efficiency of the distribution systems of oil companies has increased due to public demand increase. Consequently, in most countries, researchers and engineers focused on developing techniques for leak detection to detect pipeline leakage issues in gas and oil industries.

Manual Sound Listening

In the 1850s, the first detection method for water leakage based on listening was introduced [7]. The sounding method which is manual involves placing a wooden listening rod on the contact points of the fittings and pipeline system, like main valves. The sound generated from pressurized pipes and leaking water is detected by the listening rod. This function is similar to the stethoscope used by doctors to listen to a human heartbeat. The use of listening devices from old methods is inexpensive and straightforward. However, listening methods are more time taking and questionable effectiveness. Moreover, sound does not travel along nonmetallic pipes.

Noise Correlation Technique

In the 1970s, by the development of, the improvement in locating and detecting leaks is developed using leak noise correlation. The noise correlation technique and listening based methods are almost similar. However, the difference of this method is the use of a technique of correlation to analyze the noise detected by the sensor. In the 1980s, leak detection and monitoring systems were introduced [8].

Transient Analysis Method

From 2010, This method is used to analyze the water pipeline system with internal sensors, which are temperature, pressure and flow rate sensors [9, 10]. A V-type ultrasonic leak detection system is proposed for pipeline leak detection in [11].

The design of these transducers is to transmit ultrasonic frequency to pipeline with a resolution of around 1 Hz and 40 kHz center frequency. The reflected signal from the ultrasonic sensor measures pipeline vibration. However, to measure vibrating signals for underground pipeline systems this method is not suitable.

Fiber Optic Method

Optical fiber plays an important role in pipeline real-time monitoring and detection system where optical fibers are laid above the pipeline [12]. The external vibration induced from the pipeline can be measured by the optical fiber vibration sensor. If the pipeline vibration frequency exceeds the threshold value and the existence of any fiber damages system triggers an alarm and at the same time locate the damage site. Moreover, further damage can be prevented by maintenance workers.

Based on fiber optic approaches, several pipeline leakage detection systems have been addressed in [25, 26-28]. Utilizing distributed optical fiber for pipeline leak detection has been addressed in [29].

Acoustic Emission Sensors

According to the American Society of Mechanical Engineering (ASME) 316 standard [13], Acoustic emission is a phenomenon where elastic waves are employed. It generates 1 MHz range of frequencies at the time of the leaks [14] that allows one to detect pipeline leakage can also be detected incidents due to high-pressure fluid escaping from the perforated point [15]. To identify the leakage position, the time lag between the acoustic signals sensed by two sensors is employed [16]. Two classes of acoustic methods for leak detection are addressed which are passive and active methods [17]. Geophone, aquaphones and acoustic correlation technique are three major categories of acoustic sensors. Aquaphones require direct contact with valves, where geophones listen to leak sounds on the surface directly above the pipeline. To transmit signals, steel inserted into the pipe which buried to mount sensors on the rods. However, Due to their slow functioning procedures, these approaches are not very much effective [18]. By using pattern recognition and acoustic emission methods socket joint failure is observed experimentally which leads to pipeline leaks [19].

Accelerometers

Accelerometers are one type of vibroacoustic measuring device which are useful to monitor vibrations of the pipe shell with low frequency [20]. Using accelerometers there are several studies were addressed in achieving leak detection and localization. [21, 22]. Wireless accelerometers are utilized to detect pipeline leakage issues on the exterior of valves which connects pipeline networks that are addressed in [21]. The usage of both hydrophones and accelerometers for monitoring pipelines was addressed in [23, 24].

Vapour Sampling Method

Vapour sampling is suitable to determine gas discharges into the environment surrounding the pipeline. The tube is filled with air and pressure-dependent on atmospheric pressure. Oil spillage can be determined by measuring the recorded gas concentration as a function of the pumping time for thus the degree of absorption [30]. In the events of pipeline leakages, gas or vapor diffuses into the tube as a result of concentration gradient which, after a certain time will result from an accumulated signal indicating hydrocarbon flit in the tube environment [31].

The leak peak increases when the gas concentration increases. The higher the gas concentration in the tube surrounding, the more the leak peak increases.

Types of vapor sampling-based pipeline leak monitoring systems have been suggested by the author in [32, 33].

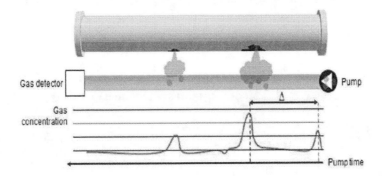

Figure 4. Sensor hose system for pipeline leakage detection [34].

Infrared Thermography

The mechanism of infrared thermography (IRT) for pipeline leakage detection systems applies to the detection of leakages in the pipeline system. IRT is an infrared image-based technique that uses infrared cameras to detect variations in temperature in the pipeline system environment [30].

The capturing of the image using an IR thermography camera is called as a thermogram. A thermography camera functioning is shown in Figure 5.

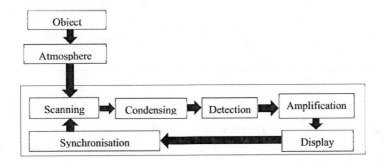

Figure 5. Basic functions of an IR thermography camera [35].

Ground Penetration Radar

The technology behind GPR which is an environmental system is especially useful to give aid to mine detection efforts which can be traced back to 1960 [36].

GPR is an instrument which is non-invasive high resolution utilized for scattering techniques and propagation of electromagnetic wave to detect alterations in the electrical and magnetic properties of the soil in the pipeline surroundings [37].

Table 2. Comparison of leak detection methods from various references

Methods	Principle of operations	Strengths	Limitations
Mass-volume Balance [44, 45]	To find the leaks it takes similarity between downstream and upstream mass volume of a fluid	Low cost, straightforward, not sensitive to noise interference and portable	Leak size-dependent, not useful for leak localization.
Negative Pressure Wave [46, 47]	Utilizes negative waves generated due to pressure propagated due to pressure drops because of pipeline leaks	Suitable for leak localization and Response time is good	This method is effective for large leaks.
Pressure Point Analysis [42, 43]	It works on the principle of monitoring pressure of starting and ending pipeline system valves.	Appropriate for cold climates, underwater environments andadequately functioning under diverse flow conditions.	When pipeline valves are opened and closed simultaneously, then leak detection is quite challenging.
Digital Signal Processing[48]	To gather data this method extracts various signal features like amplitude, The coefficients of the wavelet transform, etc.	Useful to detect and locate pipeline leaks.	Easily prone to false alarms.
Dynamic Modeling [49. 50]	Leaks information can be detected by using the similarity of simulated values based on the equation of state for the fluid and data measured	This is applicable for fast and more information can be handled for leak detection andlocalization.	Computational complexity is high and expensive
State Estimation[51]	Estimates the missing variablesusing a set of algebraic equations that relates a set of State variables, output, and input.	Very Suitable for estimating themissing variable and reconstruction of thestate vector.	The cons vary based onestimator classes such as discarding of uncertainties during simulation, computational complexity, and poor convergence factors etc.

Fluorescence Method

To detect hydrocarbon spill fluorescence methods gives light sources of a particular wavelength for excitation of molecule in the substance which is targeted to a higher energy level [38].

The occurrence of hydrocarbon spillage (unfiltered ultraviolet) light leakage detection using fluorescent dyes has been successfully implemented [39].

Capacitive Sensing

This Capacitive sensing technique is used to identify the existence of hydrocarbon spillage by changes in the dielectric constant of the medium surrounding the sensor [40]. Considering the leak size, the sensitivity of the sensor is dependent on the distance between the position of a leak and the drift of the leaking medium [41].

3. PROPOSED METHODOLOGY FOR PIPELINE LEAKAGE MONITORING

Figure 6 shows the pipeline leak monitoring system.

These two pressure meters are placed on the pipeline valves which are used to measure the pipeline pressure.

Moreover, two accelerometer sensors are placed above the pipeline to measure vibrations of the pipeline.

These two parameter sensors embedded with the LoRa transmitters to send the sensed data to a safe operation controller and end-user i.e., application server.

Here LoRa (Long Range) is one of the communication protocols which capable to transmit and receive data up to 15 kilometers. The main advantage of this protocol is its focus on long-range data communication with less power consumption.

The received data from the sensors will be communicated to Servers via LoRa gateway.

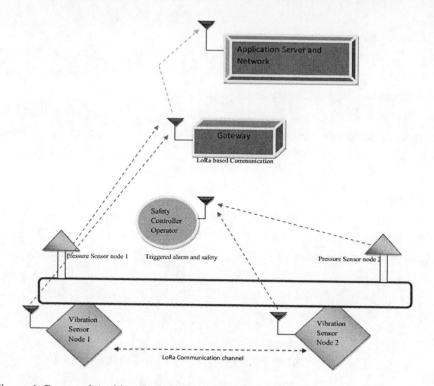

Figure 6. Proposed Architecture of Pipeline Leakage Monitoring System.

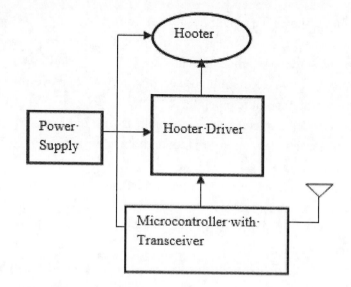

Figure 7. Safety Operation controller.

3.1. Safety Operation Controller (SOC)

Figure 7 addresses the safety operation controller (SOC) which plays a prominent role in alerting, monitoring staff and others from fire accidents across the pipeline system. When vibration sensors and pressure sensors give abnormal values of the pipeline the data will be sent to the safe operation controller via LoRa gateway and microcontroller. This controller receives information and activates hooter through a hooter driver.

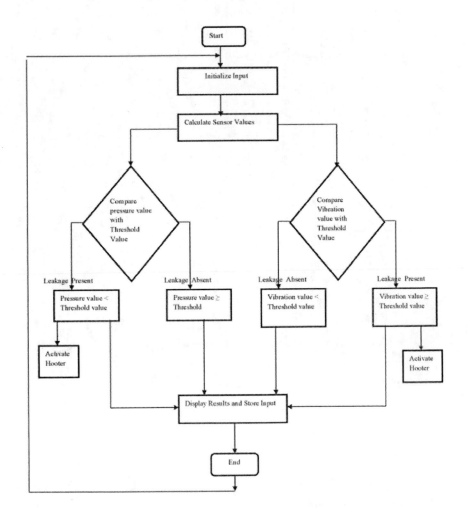

Figure 8. Flow chart.

CONCLUSION

This paper provides information about various leak detection technologies. Various pipeline leak detection methods and techniques were grouped and reviewed. The methods look attentively in this category includes infrared thermography, acoustic emission, vapor sampling, optic sensors, and ground penetration radar. The advantages and limitations of leakage detection such as negative pressure waves, mass-volume balance, and digital signal processing, dynamic modeling and pressure point analysis were addressed. Furthermore, the methodology and architecture of the pipeline monitoring system using the Lure and IoT network were proposed.

REFERENCES

[1]   Wang, T., W. Xuan, X. Wang et al. "Overview of oil and gas pipeline failure database", in *Proceedings of International Conference on Pipelines and Trenchless Technology, ICPTT,* 2013, pp.1161 - 1167, chn, October 2013.

[2]   Peng, X., D. Yao, G. Liang, J. Yu and S. He. Overall reliability analysis on oil/gas pipeline under typical third-party actions based on fragility theory, {*Journal of Natural Gas Science and Engineering*}, Vol. 34 (Aug. 31), pp. 993 - 1003, 2016.

[3]   Lianshuang Dai,1,2 Dongpo Wang,1 Ting Wang,3 Qingshan Feng,2 and Xinqi Yang,"Analysis and Comparison of Long-Distance Pipeline Failures", *Journal of Petroleum Engineering Volume,* 2017, Article ID 3174636.

[4]   PHMSA, http://primis.phmsa.dot.gov/comm/reports/safety/PSI .html. 2015.

[5]   EGIG, "9th report of the gas pipeline incidents of European gas pipeline incident data group", 2015.

[6]   UKOPA, "UKOPA pipeline product loss incidents and faults report (1962–2014)", 2015.

[7]   Zhang, J. "Designing a cost-effective and reliable pipeline leak-detection system",*Pipes and Pipelines International*, vol. 42, no. 1, pp. 20 - 26, 1997.

[8]   Covas, D., H. Ramos and A. B. de Almeida. "Standing Wave Difference Method for Leak Detection in Pipeline Systems",*Journal of Hydraulic Engineering,* vol. 131, no. 12, pp. 1106 - 1116, dec. 2005.

[9]   Ghazali, M. F., P. S. B. M. B. Staszewski and P. W. J. "Leak Detection Using Instantaneous Frequency Analysis", Ph.D. dissertation, Sheffield, 2012.

[10]   Ghazali, M., W. Staszewski, J. Shucksmith, J. Boxall and S. Beck. "Instantaneous phase and frequency for the detection of leaks and features in a pipeline system",*StructuralHealth Monitoring,* vol. 10, no. 4, pp. 351 - 360, jun. 2010.

[11]   Chamran,M. K. and S. Shafie. "A Non-Invasive Air-Coupled V-Type Ultrasonic Leak Detection System", may 2015. [Online]. Available: https://www.sign-ific-ance.co.uk/index.php/PURE/article/ view/884.

[12]   Guo, X., Zhang, L., Liang, W., Haugen, S. Risk identification of third-party damage on oil and gas pipelines through the Bayesian network, *Journal of Loss Prevention in the Process Industries,*(2018), doi: 10.1016/j.jlp.2018.03.012.

[13]   ASTME1316-16a. *Standard Terminology for Nondestructive Examinations*; ASTM International:West Conshohocken, PA, USA, 2016.

[14]   Martini, A., Troncossi, M., Rivola, A. Leak Detection in Water-Filled Small-Diameter Polyethylene Pipes by Means of Acoustic Emission Measurements. *Appl. Sci.,*2017, 7, 2.

[15]   Cramer, R., Shaw, D., Tulalian, R., Angelo, P., Van Stuijvenberg, M. Detecting and correcting pipeline leaks before they become a big problem. *Mar. Technol. Soc. J.,*2015, 49, 31 - 46.

[16]   Li, S., Wen, Y., Li, P., Yang, J., Yang, L. Leak detection and location for gas pipelines using acoustic emission sensors. In *Proceedings of the 2012 IEEE International Ultrasonics Symposium (IUS),* Dresden, Germany, 7 - 10 October 2012; *IEEE*: Piscataway, NJ, USA, 2012; pp. 957 - 960.

[17] Recommended, Practice. DNVL-RP-F302—Edition April 2016. Available online: https://rules.dnvgl.com/docs/pdf/DNVGL/RP/2016-04/DNVGL-RP-F302.pdf.

[18] Chatzigeorgiou, D., Youcef-Toumi, K., Ben-Mansour, R. Design of a novel in-pipe reliable leak detector.*IEEE/ASME Trans. Mechatron,*2015, 20, 824 - 833.

[19] Li, S., Song, Y., Zhou, G. Leak detection of water distribution pipeline subject to failure of socket joint based on acoustic emission and pattern recognition. *Measurement,*2018, 115, 39 - 44.

[20] Yazdekhasti, S., Piratla, K.R., Atamturktur, S., Khan, A. Novel vibration-based technique for detection of water pipeline leakage. *Struct. Infrastruct. Eng.,*2017, 13, 731 - 742.

[21] El-Zahab, S., Mohammed Abdelkader, E., Zayed, T. An accelerometer-based leak detection system. *Mech. Syst. Signal Process,*2018, 108, 58 - 72.

[22] Yazdekhasti, S., Piratla, K.R., Atamturktur, S., Khan, A. Experimental evaluation of a vibration-based leak detection technique for water pipelines. *Struct. Infrastruct. Eng.,*2018, 14,46 - 55.

[23] Martini, A., Troncossi, M., Rivola, A. Vibroacoustic Measurements for Detecting Water Leaks in Buried Small-Diameter Plastic Pipes. *J. Pipeline Syst. Eng. Pract.,*2017, 8, 1 - 10.

[24] Martini, A., Rivola, A., Troncossi, M. Autocorrelation Analysis of Vibro-Acoustic Signals Measured in a Test Field for Water Leak Detection. *Appl. Sci.,*2018, 8, 2450.

[25] Jia, Z., Wang, Z., Sun, W., Li, Z. Pipeline leakage localization based on distributed FBG hoop strain measurements and support vector machine. *Optik,*2019, 176, 1 - 13.

[26] Khan, A.A., Vrabie, V., Mars, J.I., Girard, A., D'Urso, G. A source separation technique for processing of thermometric data from fibre-optic DTS measurements for water leakage identification in dikes. *IEEE Sens. J.,* 2008, 8, 1118 - 1129.

[27] Kroll, A., Baetz, W., Peretzki, D. On autonomous detection of pressured air and gas leaks using passive IR-thermography for mobile robot application. In *Proceedings of the IEEE International*

Conference on Robotics and Automation, 2009 (ICRA'09), Kobe, Japan, 12–17 May 2012; *IEEE*: Piscataway, NJ, USA, 2009; pp. 921 - 926.

[28] Zhang, S., Liu, B., He, J. Pipeline deformation monitoring using distributed fibre optical sensor. *Measurement,*2019, 133, 208 - 213.

[29] Du, J., Wang, L., Cai, C., Yin, C., Zhao, G. Study on distributed optical fibre heating pipeline network leak detection system. In *Proceedings of the 2017 IEEE 2nd Information Technology, Networking, Electronic and Automation Control Conference (ITNEC),* Chegdu, China, 15–17 December 2017; *IEEE:* Piscataway, NJ, USA, 2017; pp. 137 - 140.

[30] Golmohamadi, M. *Pipeline Leak Detection.* Master's Thesis, Missouri University of Science and Technology,Rolla, MO, USA, 2015.

[31] Geiger, G., Vogt, D., Tetzner, R. State-of-the-art in leak detection and localization. *Oil Gas Eur. Mag.,*2006,32, 1 - 26.

[32] Murvay, P., Silea, I. A survey on gas leak detection and localization techniques. *J. Loss Prev. Process Ind.,*2012, 25, 966 - 973.

[33] Ahmed, M., Shama, A., Mohamed, E., Mohamed, K. Review of leakage detection methods for subsea pipeline. *Arab Acad. Sci. Technol. Marit. Transp.,*2017, 1, 1 - 9.

[34] Boaz, L., Kaijage, S., Sinde, R. An overview of pipeline leak detection and location systems. In *Proceedings of the 2nd Pan African International Conference on Science, Computing and Telecommunications (PACT 2014),* Arusha, Tanzania, 14–18 July 2014; *IEEE:* Piscataway, NJ, USA, 2014.

[35] Manekiya, M.H., Arulmozhivarman, P. Leakage detection and estimation using IR thermography. In *Proceedings of the 2016 International Conference on Communication and Signal Processing (ICCSP),* Melmaruvathur, India, 6–8 April 2016; *IEEE*: Piscataway, NJ, USA, 2016; pp. 1516 - 1519.

[36] Bimpas, M., Amditis, A., Uzunoglu, N. Detection of water leaks in supply pipes using continuous wave sensor operating at 2.45 GHz. *J. Appl. Geophys.,*2010, 70, 226 - 236.

[37] Adedeji, K.B., Hamam, Y., Abe, B.T., Abu-Mahfouz, A.M. Towards achieving a reliable leakage detection and localization algorithm for

application in water piping networks: An overview. *IEEE Access,* 2017, 5, 20272 - 20285.

[38] Recommended, Practice. DNVL-RP-F302—Edition April 2016. Available online: https://rules.dnvgl.com/docs/pdf/DNVGL/RP/2016-04/DNVGL-RP-F302.pdf.

[39] Jasper, A. Oil/Gas Pipeline Leak Inspection and Repair in Underwater Poor Visibility Conditions: Challenges and Perspectives. *J. Environ. Prot.,* 2012, 3, 394 - 399.

[40] Recommended, Practice. DNVL-RP-F302—Edition April 2016. Available online: https://rules.dnvgl.com/docs/pdf/DNVGL/RP/2016-04/DNVGL-RP-F302.pdf (accessed on 15 February 2019).

[41] Recommended Practice, DNV-RP-F302. Selection and Use of Subsea Leak Detection Systems. April 2010. Available online: https://rules.dnvgl.com/docs/pdf/DNV/codes/docs/2010-04/RP-F302.pdf (accessed on 20 February 2019).

[42] Bin, M. D., Akib, A., Bin Saad, N., Asirvadam, V. Pressure point analysis for early detection system. In *Proceedings of the 2011 IEEE 7th International Colloquium on Signal Processing and its Applications (CSPA),* Penang, Malaysia, 4–6 March 2011; *IEEE*: Piscataway, NJ, USA, 2011; pp. 103 - 107.

[43] Arifin, B., Li, Z., Shah, S.L., Meyer, G.A., Colin, A. A novel data-driven leak detection and localization algorithm using the Kantorovich distance. *Comput. Chem. Eng.,* 2018, 108, 300 - 313.

[44] Ostapkowicz, P. Leak detection in liquid transmission pipelines using simplified pressure analysis techniques employing a minimum of standard and non-standard measuring devices. *Eng. Struct.,* 2016, 113, 194 - 205.

[45] Sheltami, T. R., Bala, A., Shakshuki, E. M. Wireless sensor networks for leak detection in pipelines: A survey. *J. Ambient Intell. Humaniz. Comput.,* 2016, 7, 347 - 356.

[46] Sang, Y., Zhang, J., Lu, X., Fan, Y. Signal processing based on wavelet transform in pipeline leakage detection and location. In *Proceedings of the Sixth International Conference on Intelligent Systems Design*

and Applications (ISDA '06), Jinan, China, 16–18 October 2006; *IEEE*: Piscataway, NJ, USA, 2006; pp. 734 - 739. [CrossRef].

[47] Yu, Z., Jian, L., Zhoumo, Z., Jin, S. A combined kalman filter-Discrete wavelet transform method for leakage detection of crude oil pipelines. In *Proceedings of the 9th International Conference on Electronic Measurement and Instruments (ICEMI '09),* Beijing, China, 16–19 August 2009; *IEEE:* Piscataway, NJ, USA, 2009; pp. 3-1086 - 3-1090.

[48] Lay-Ekuakille, A., Vergallo, P., Trotta, A. Impedance method for leak detection in zigzag pipelines. *Meas. Sci. Rev.,* 2010, 10, 209 - 213.

[49] He, G., Liang, Y., Li, Y., Wu, M., Sun, L., Xie, C., Li, F. A method for simulating the entire leaking process and calculating the liquid leakage volume of a damaged pressurized pipeline. *J. Hazard. Mater.,* 2017, 332, 19 - 32.

[50] Yang, Z., Fan, S., Xiong, T. Simulation and Numerical Calculation on Pipeline Leakage Process. In *Proceedings of the 2010 2nd International Symposium on Information Engineering and Electronic Commerce (IEEC),* Ternopil, Ukraine, 23–25 July 2010; *IEEE*: Piscataway, NJ, USA, 2010; pp. 1 - 5.

[51] Besançon, G. Observer tools for pipeline monitoring. In *Modeling and Monitoring of Pipelines and Networks*; Springer: Cham, Switzerland, 2017; pp. 83 - 97.

In: LoRA and IoT Networks …
Editors: A. Gehlot, R. Singh et al.

ISBN: 978-1-53617-164-8
© 2020 Nova Science Publishers, Inc.

Chapter 2

LoRaWAN: A Communication Protocol for IoT Agriculture Applications

Mahendra Swain, Rajesh Singh[†], Anita Gehlot[‡] and Md. Farukh Hashmi[§]*

Department of Electronics and Communication Engineering,
Lovely Professional University, Punjab,
National Institute of Technology, Warangal

ABSTRACT

This chapter illustrates, how Low power wide area networks (LPWA) are becoming very popular nowadays because of their low power uses and wide area coverage. A survey of a recent article published included areas of Low Power Wide Area networks and their applications. An overview of LoRa architecture along with communication technique used in it has been

---

[*] Corresponding Author's Email: er.mahendraswain@gmail.com.
[†] Corresponding Author's Email: srajssssece@gmail.com.
[‡] Corresponding Author's Email: eranita5@gmail.com.
[§] Corresponding Author's Email: mdfarukh@nitw.ac.in.

briefly elaborated. Comparatively analysis have been done over existing techniques like NBIoT, Sigfox, WiFi, BLE, Zigbee etc. In relation to agricultural uses, here we have elaborate customized device where data gets gathered from various sensor nodes which are deployed at field and communication with receiver via LoRa network. Challenge s and opportunity has been shown at the end of this chapter. Looking to the Indian agriculture system, it has been seen that adapting this technique to the real life application could bring many of benefits to the farmer in terms of field monitoring, agricultural product quality enhancement, uses of water, soil quality and finally maximum yield of farming products. The future scope with integrating various technology like block chain has been also discussed to improve reliability and security issues involved in it.

Keywords: LoRa, IoT, LPWAN, Agriculture, NBIoT, Sigfox, WiFi, BLE, Zigbee

LITERATURE SURVEY

An intensive survey on LoRa protocols has been done. Its popularity and previous art has been noted. Low Power Wide Area Networks (LPWAN) now gaining a lot of attention because less power usages. It is so popular in industry, academia and day today applications [1, 2]. This approach has the potential to transmits the information in wide range i.e in in kms without any wire and also capable of interacting thousands of IoT devices for communication without human interference [3, 4]. Applications such as smart city, smart waste management, smart light, smart parking, smart farming etc are becoming easier with this technique. [5–6]. LoRa is battery operated on low power can be interfaced with multiple sensor and actuators to sense and control the appliances respectively [7]. It is predicted that by 2020 more than 50 billion devices will be inter connect with each other for data transfer. Technology like LoRa, NBIoT are more reliable due to its advance features over other communication protocols [1]. T This article present a literature review of fifty suitable article, where the application area, categorization of LoRa and finally some recommendations are provided for the uses of this network. Where researcher could have idea to develop solutions using LoRa on IoT platform. [6]The revolution of future technology like 5G also came in to the as far as the communication with a great speed is concerned. Now a days communication protocols are being designed to prevent security issues. LPWAN playa very crucial role to eradicate this kinds of issue related to security [12]. A multi hop LoRaWAN based architecture has been developed for the underground automation. Challenges including blind spot detection, where there is no signal has been identified and solution has been given to eradicate these connectivity issues in it [13]. The worldview of Internet of Things (IoT) is making ready for a world, where a considerable lot of our day by day items will be interconnected and will interface with their condition so as to gather data and computerize certain assignments. Such a dream requires, in addition to other things, consistent validation, information protection, security, strength against assaults, simple arrangement, and self-support. World population will be nine billion by 2050. Many challenges are faced due to less land and demand of agricultural product increment. So, agriculture farming technique need to be replace by modern technique in order to achieve this goals [14]. This paper surveyed various articles on suitable agriculture monitoring technologies for precision agriculture using IoT platform. Cloud based technique has been discussed for sensor monitoring and control [17]. A cloud enabled architecture has been implemented using various cloud platform to facilitate easy end user application. Analytical tools has been engaged for analysis of various parameter to choose suitable communication protocol over IoT framework [19]. TI CC3200 Launchpad based sensor nodes devices has been developed for ICT agricultural sector looking towards the challenge faced by Indian farmers. The cost effectiveness of this device has many more advantages than the exciting devices. Special emphasis have been given to reduce labor cost and water resourse management for agro farms [21-24]. Looking towards the current population growth and reducing farming lands, coming challenges and solution has been studied in this article [25]. IoT platform supported solution has been developed for farmer in this article. Further it describes the future scope using integrating various cloud platforms for the same [27]. At the same time Cloud Computing, which is already very popular, and Fog Computing provide sufficient resources and solutions to sustain, store and analyses the huge amounts of data generated by IoT devices [28]. This article presents, a comparative study on IoT and cloud based platform from various prospective like quality of service and connectivity [29]. In this article, a technical survey of various IoT technologies has been mentioned. Further it describe the looking towards the required application development to select the best suit technique like LoRa, NBIoT, Sigfox. With respect to this following parameters like distance coverage, battery life, scalability and cost has been discussed [30].

INTRODUCTION

LoRa (brief for long range) is a popular communication protocol used in IoT platform. It is derived from Chirp Spread Spectrum, a modulation spectrum technique. LoRaWAN is very power efficient communication technicque and cover wide area for communication over wireless channel. Generally this is battery operated and connect to nearby devices with a distance of 2 to 3 kilometers as mentioned by LoRa alliance. LoRa is operated with a frequency band of 433/470/868/780/915 MHz ISM bands. It makes a bridge among other communication protocols like BLE, WiFi, GPRS etc. LoRaWAN is capable to overcome obstacle came in between transmitter and receiver with better efficiency. It follows star topology where gateways and server are linked with each other over IP connections. Here, RF packet data is converted in to IP packet and vice versa. The arrangement could to one to many, many to one and many to many via hop link. All nodes connected to this network are responsible for both transmission and reception of information. The battery operated nodes are have good battery life and wide range connectivity. LoRa is more suitable for remotely operated applications where sensor nodes or devices are deployed at a distance. LoRa was developed Cycleo of Grenoble,France later in 2012 it was acquired by Semtech company. The advance features of this technology make it more popular and widely deployed with IoT devices compare to Wi-Fi which is operated at 2.4 GHz. Although there is certain limitation in LoRa in terms data transfer rate. The bitrate of LoRa is less than Wi-Fi is around 20 to 30 Kbps.

LoRa Key Features

- Cover a long range of communication distance around 10 to 15km line of sight and 2 to 5 with obstacle in between
- No restricted number of nodes get connected over LoRa network it could be 1 million nodes
- Maintain a long battery life up to 10 years as per claimed by Semtech
- Network synchronization is easy and no hops in LoRaWAN
- LoRa is more secure and reliable
- Immune toward noise or interference in network over wireless channel
- Low cost device
- Customized architecture can be designed as per specific application example for agriculture.

The above features differentiate from others and make it more popular. Research on IoT So Far:

In last few years the impact of Low-Power Wide Area Networks (LPWAN) has been observed in industry and academia. Industry is more focused to drive LoRa based application which could be more beneficial for human society. [1, 2] The LoRa based IoT ecosystem provides a multidimensional application in various domains. LoRa architecture consists of sensor node which is recognized as End devices, Gateway which establish communication link between end devices and server. Server store all information locally which could be updated on cloud later stage. [3, 4]. It has been predicted that by 2020 more than twenry five billion devices will be connected wirelessly and interact among themselves. In this context, we can imagine role of this technology which can drive whole society in to different level of expectation. There are many communication protocols used now days. LoRa secure its position in terms of distance covered and low power consumption. Figure 1. Shows a various communication protocols with distance covered and power consumption in mW. We can take example of BLE, which is very popular communication protocol having a good quality data transfer rate within 10 to 15 feets. BLE been seen in almost all devices including Smart phones, earphones, speakers etc. Similarly WiFi is there, but LoRa win the race.

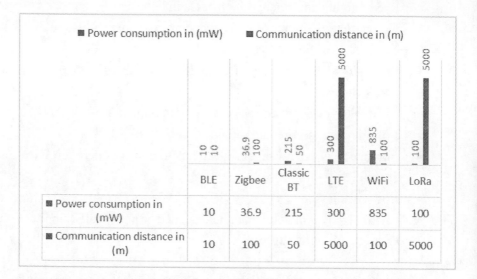

	BLE	Zigbee	Classic BT	LTE	WiFi	LoRa
■ Power consumption in (mW)	10	36.9	215	300	835	100
■ Communication distance in (m)	10	100	50	5000	100	5000

Figure 1. Comparison popular communication protocols used day today.

Now let s move to architecture of LoRa .

ARCHITECTURE OF LoRaWAN

The architecture of LoRa comprise of

    i.   End node devices
   ii.   Gateway
  iii.   Network Server
  iv.   Application Layer
   v.   End nodes:

These are the sensor nodes deployed in field. Example pH sensor, temperature, humidity sensors which are interfaced to the controller of the node and transmits information from field. End nodes can be changed as per required application. End nodes could exchange information to the server via gateway.

Gateway: This is the intermediate network between end devices and server. Gateway are nothing but the routers connected locally to each other. Each device connect with unique id to the gateway.

Network Server: Network server store all authenticated information collected from sensor nodes. It process the data and identify the required one using data analytics. Network server interconnect with gateway via ethernet cable or over WiFi.

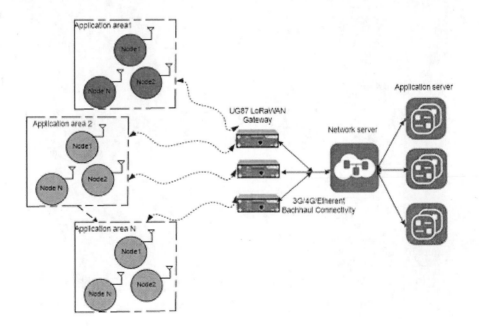

Fgure 2. LoRa architecture.

Application Layer: These are final stage of this architecture where application interface control all the activities at sensor nodes. etc. It facilitate number of features like virtual terminal, web services, email, file transfer etc. It could be any interface, GUI (Graphical User Interface), Mobile apps etc. Like MQTT, Blynk.This layer directly interacts with user. It focus on machine to machine or process to process communication.

Synchronization and Scheduling for LoRaWAN

ADR(Adaptive Data Rate) system and distinctive SFs control appropriation will improve arrange adaptability in LoRaWAN. In any case, still the principle organize versatility bottleneck is utilization of Aloha based MAC convention. What's more, the half-duplex activity of passages just as obligation cycle restriction expanded the negative effect on system adaptability.

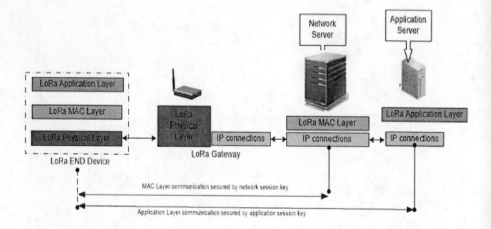

Figure 3. LoRa Gateway.

In LoRa architecture, nodes are interconnected with star-to star topology.It supports three various endpoint classes. These are listed below.

a.   Class A
b.   Class B
c.   Class C

Class A: It is a bidirectional device connected at end node. Both transmission and reception is possible in this class. In order to do this end devices are provided with uplink and downlink windows. One is for transmission and another is for reception. Transfer occurs through some dedicated time slots assigned by the user. Uplink transmission helps send the data from end devices to the server and downlink wait until the data gets received. This consume very less power to enhance battery efficiency.

Class B: It is superior to Class A end device. It does have bi-directional end-devices along with received slot which follow scheduled mechanism. It has an extra receive window which looks after time slots allocated at uplink window. Proper synchronization is maintained between gateway and end devices to ensure, gateway listen to end device .i.e all data received at gateway.

Class C:It does have the features of Class A and with maximum receiving slots. This class of LoRa network support reception window with regular reception of data from end devices. This class C is preferred when large amount of data need to be received at gateway. Class C close its window during transmission only.

Message Passing over LoRa

Message passing over LoRaWAN is very crucial, when end devices pass message to gateway in coverage network area. It receives the message and acknowledgement signal passed to the devices. To design cost effective network, adapting localization algorithm used. Minimum number of devices can be deployed to collect the data. Gateways approves the received data, which are coming from end devices. This way error can be reduced in the LoRa network. Several layers of encryption has been done to keep the data secure. These are listed below:

- Unique Network key (EUI64) : It is responsible to keep the data safe and secure when data passes through various networks

- Unique Application key (EUI64) : This key takes care of the data when data transmits from one node to another in application layer of LoRa network
- Specific key for end device (EUI128): Device dedicated keys make authentication of devices connected to LoRa network wirelessly. Each device allocated with a specific key.

Working:

Transmission symbol rate in LoRa network calculated using following formula.

$$Symbol\ rate\ (Rs) = S.F * \frac{BW}{2^{S.F}}$$

where   S. F is the spreading factor in LoRa network;
        BW: Bandwidth in Hertz.

LoRa Frame structure

Data transmission occurs in LoRa follow data frame structure mentioned in above Figure 4. Preamble is the program code need to be transferred. PHY header mechanism applied to the data packets. CRC is the cyclic redundancy check take care of the same correct data bits received. Payload contain LoRa WAN or MAC data bits.

Figure 4. Data frame in LoRa.

LoRa Simulation Platforms

There are various LoRa simulators are there which can be used to simulate the data Table 1 Shows simulators support different platforms and code.

Platform	Uplink	Downlink	MAC Commands	Downlink traffic	Physical Model
NS3	YES	YES	NO	YES	All interface based
Python	NO	NO	NO	NO	Power difference based
C++	YES	NO	NO	NO	

Simulator features has been mentioned in Table 1 with respect to physical model designed in the simulator.

Block Diagram

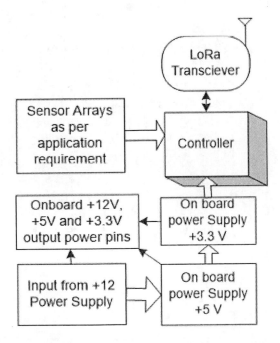

Figure 5. Block diagram for LoRa based transmitter.

The block diagram of LoRa transmitter has been shown in Figure 5. It comprises of power supply unit both 5 Volt and 12 volt variants. ATMEGA 328 Controller has been used in this transmitter and custom fabricated on PCB(Printed Circuit Board). There are multiple pins dedicated for sensor interfacing both analog and digital sensors like pH. Ultrasonic, temperature, humidity, pressure sensor, rain fall sensor, gas sensors etc. Controller has been interfaced with LoRa module. The data coming from sensors get transmitted to nearest local gateway.

END Device

The block diagram consists of power supply unit. On board power supply pins +5 Volt, +12 Volts. ATMEGA 328 has been interfaced with Liquid Crystal display where all data can be visualized. LoRa module has been interfaced to transmit the data.

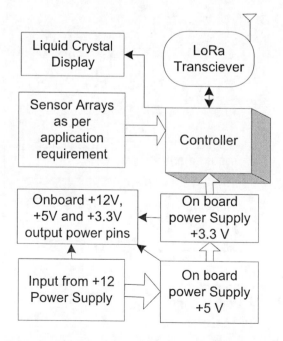

Figure 6. Block diagram for LoRa based end device.

Receiver

LoRa receiver is meant for receiving all the information from transmitter module. LoRa receiver module transfer information to gateway.

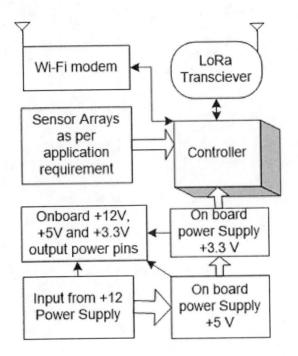

Figure 7. Block diagram for LoRa based receiver.

LoRa Gateway

LoRa gateway is the intermediator between transmitter and receiver module. It receive the data from transmitter and pass the information to the receiver. The block diagram has power supply unit, meant for power supply +5Volts, +12Volts. Sensor array for interfacing sensor nodes. Controller interfaced relay module to connect AC (Alternating Current) operated devices/Machines like water pump, blower, sprinkler etrc.

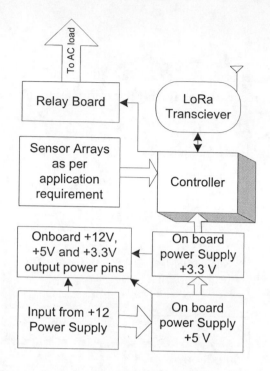

Figure 8. Block diagram for LoRa gateway.

Hardware Platform

A customized LoRa test bed has been designed to validate test code. Figure 9. Shows LoRa customized transmitter module. It has dedicated analog and digital pins to interface various sensors to it. It is treated as end device in reference to LoRa architecture. It is operated on rechargeable battery and can be deployed in to the agriculture field for field monitoring. The LoRa module has been fabricated with ATMEGA328P. PCB design for the same has been done pcb trace software.

The circuit diagram shown in above Figure 10 is for LoRa transmitter. The detail circuit diagram has been elaborated below. It comprises of ATMEGA328 microcontroller, power supply unit, LoRa modem, sensor array strip for interfacing various sensors.

Figure 9. Customized LoRa end device node.

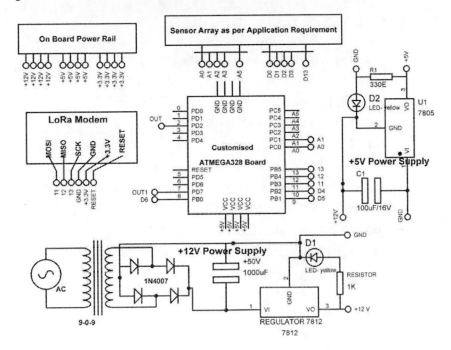

Figure 10. Circuit for LoRa Transmitter node.

ATMEGA328 is a high end 8-bit RISC microcontroller having 32KB of ISP flash memory with read and write capability, 23 general purpose input output lines and 10-bit ADC. Controller operates voltage between 1.8 to 5

Volts [31]. Power supply unit consists of 9-0-9 AC step down transformer along with bridge rectifier consists of four IN4007 diodes. The output voltage then passed through the regulated with regulated ICs (LM7812, LM7805). LM7812 is very low cost positive voltage regulator IC yield 12 Volt output. It has three terminals IN, COM and OUT. IN is for input, COM is for ground and OUT is to get the output from IC. An indicator has been connected to check the power supply unit working status. Whereas LM7805 is a positive voltage regulator IC with 5 Volt output voltage. Both of these IC belomg from same 78xx IC family.

LoRa modem SX1278 is a transceiver manufactured by SEMTECH with different operating frequencies from 137MHz to 525MHz with low power consumption. The features of LoRa modem has been mentioned below:

- 168dB link budget in LoRa
- +20dBm - 100mW constant RF output vs. V supply
- +14dBm high efficiency PA
- Transmission bit rate 300kbps
- Immunity towards Noise interference
- Low Receiver current 9.9mA, 200nA retention in register
- FSK, GFSK, MSK, GMSK, LoRa and OOK modulation
- Built-in bit synchronizer for clock recovery
- Automatic RF Sense and CAD with ultra-fast AFC
- Data packet rate up to 256 bytes with CRC
- Low battery indicator and temperature sensor is inbuilt on modem

LoRa modem has been interfaced to ATMEGA328 with MOSI,MISO, SCLK and ground. Sesnsor array having multiple analog and digital pins to interface with digital and analog sensors like DHT11, rainfall sensor, soil pH sensor, soil humidity sensor, pressure sensor and gas sensors etc.

In Figure 10 both transmitter and receiver module has been shown. Receiver node has LoRa module interface with 16x4 LCD to visualize sensor data from transmitting node. There are eight control buttons are there on it, to control various actuators connected to transmitter node.

Figure 10. Customized LoRa transmitter and receiver with LCD.

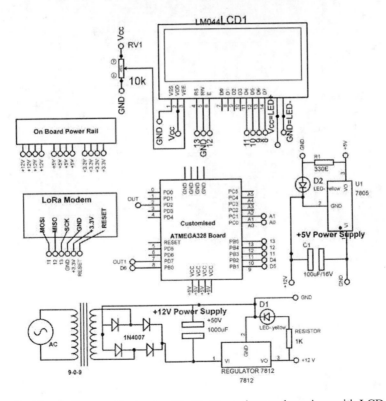

Figure 11. Circuit diagram Customized LoRa transmitter and receiver with LCD.

LoRa receiver circuit consists of ATMEGA328 controller. The description details has been given in Figure 8. Receiver module has comprises of ATMEGA328 controller and LCD of 32x4 . LoRa modem interfaced to controller with Serial to Parallel interface. Receiver LoRa modem receive the data in terms of message packet information. The module also indicate the RSSI with dbs.

Figure 12 Shows the circuit diagram of LoRa gateway .NodeMCU has been shown in the block diagram. The data could be updated in to cloud platforms by the help of this module. NodeMCU is an open source IoT platform having GPIO, PWM, ADC and inbuilt ESP 8266 WiFi module on it.

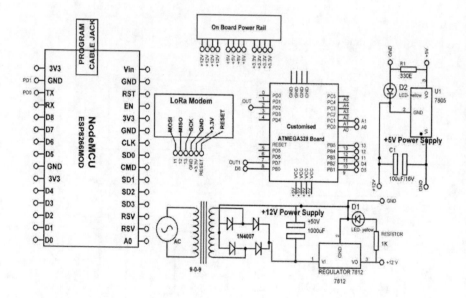

Figure 12. Circuit diagram Customized LoRa Gateway.

Programming of LoRa:
Coding for LoRa module Sender
#include <SPI.h>
#include <LoRa.h>

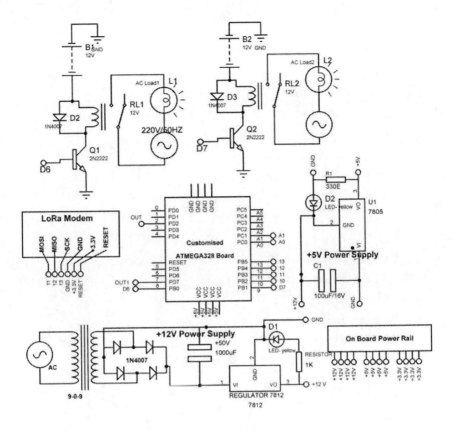

Figure 13. Circuit diagram Customized LoRa to control relays.

```
//define the pins used by the transceiver module
#define ss 10
#define rst 9
#define dio0 2

int counter = 0;
void setup() {
//initialize Serial Monitor
Serial.begin(9600);
while (!Serial);
Serial.println("LoRa Sender Tested ");
```

```
//setup LoRa transceiver module
LoRa.setPins(ss, rst, dio0);
// LoRa.begin(433E6);
//replace the LoRa.begin(---E-) argument with your location's
frequency
//433E6 for Asia
//866E6 for Europe
//915E6 for North America
if (!LoRa.begin(433E6)) {
Serial.println("Starting LoRa failed!");
while (1);
}
// Change sync word (0xF3) to match the receiver
// The sync word assures you don't get LoRa messages from other LoRa
transceivers
// ranges from 0-0xFF
LoRa.setSyncWord(0xF3);
Serial.println("LoRa Initializing OK!");
}

void loop() {
Serial.print("Sending packet: ");
Serial.println(counter);
//Send LoRa packet to receiver
LoRa.beginPacket();
LoRa.print("hello ");
LoRa.print(counter);
LoRa.endPacket();

counter++;

delay(5000);
}
```

LoRa Receiver:

```
#include<LiquidCrystal.h>
#include <SPI.h>
#include <LoRa.h>
LiquidCrystal lcd(19,18,17,16,15,14);

//define the pins used by the transceiver module
#define ss 10
#define rst 9
#define dio0 2

int counter = 0;

void setup() {
//initialize Serial Monitor
Serial.begin(9600); // don't change baud rate as tesed on 9600
lcd.begin(20,4);
lcd.clear();
while (!Serial);
Serial.println("LoRa Receiver Tested ");

//setup LoRa transceiver module
LoRa.setPins(ss, rst, dio0);
// LoRa.begin(433E6);
//replace the LoRa.begin(---E-) argument with your location's
frequency
//433E6 for Asia
//866E6 for Europe
//915E6 for North America
if (!LoRa.begin(433E6)) {
Serial.println("Starting LoRa failed!");
lcd.setCursor(0,0);
lcd.print("LoRa Error! ");
while (1);
```

```
}
// Change sync word (0xF3) to match the receiver
// The sync word assures you don't get LoRa messages from other LoRa
transceivers
// ranges from 0-0xFF
LoRa.setSyncWord(0xF3);
Serial.println("LoRa Initializing OK!");
lcd.setCursor(0,0);
lcd.print("LoRa is OK! ");
delay(3000);
}

void loop() {
// try to parse packet
int packetSize = LoRa.parsePacket();
if (packetSize) {
// received a packet
Serial.print("Received packet '");
lcd.setCursor(0,0);
lcd.print("Received packet");
// read packet
while (LoRa.available()) {
String LoRaData = LoRa.readString();
Serial.print(LoRaData);
lcd.setCursor(0,1);
lcd.print(LoRaData);
}

// print RSSI of packet
Serial.print("' with RSSI ");
Serial.println(LoRa.packetRssi());
lcd.setCursor(0,2);
lcd.print(" with RSSI ");
lcd.setCursor(0,3);
```

```
lcd.print(LoRa.packetRssi());
lcd.print(" ");


    }
}
```

ADFC Analysis

Advantages	Disadvantage
• Long distance coverage wirelessly • Less power consumption at end devices • Simple hardware • Allow to Customized network • Mostly applicable for monitoring application	• Less secure chance to get cyber attack • Data transmission rate is slow (0.3 -50kbps) • Network security terminates at various part of the network
Future Scope	**Challenges**
• Power consumption could be reduced in future • Scheduling of low power traffic • Integration with advance techniques like blockchain	• Two way communication is challenging • Heavy network load leads to more power consumption

Applications LoRa in Multidomain

LoRa covers a wide areas of application in various domain like agriculture, smart surveillance, smart city, smart building, and energy management etc.

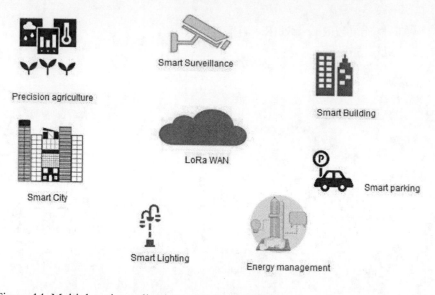

Figure 14. Multi domain application using LoRaWAN.

Smart Agriculture

Measuring of various environmental factors could bring maximum yield in the crops. Tracking of water level, soil pH, Humidity, temperature, light intensity, atmospheric presuure etc becomes very easy using LoRa network. Smart monitoring to save water, amount of fertilizers to be used and obviously to reduce the price. This facilaite the advance farming like vertical farming, hydroponic agriculture etc.

Smart Cities

Maintaining daily municipal operations has been easy using LoRaWAN. City services like parking slots, waste management, and lighting can be optimized using this network. Use of utilities can be used efficient manner which save money as well as time.

Smart Manufacturing

Factory automation requires hundreds of sensors and actuators. Collection of high precision data and measurement are very reliable usinh LoRa network. Real time monitoring using LoRa network make easy automation in industry.

Smart Building

Smart building monitoring using LoRa use more reliable due to its long battery life.

Controlling home appliances are easy with LoRa network.

CONCLUSION

Long Range communication protocol is best fit for the IoT (Internet of Things) based application. The architecture for LoRa and IoT networks has been elaborated in this chapter. We have discussed various approaches for integrating LoRa in to IoT to develop innovative solutions for Smart Building, Smart Lighting, Smart farming etc. The challenge and opportunities has been explored in ADFC chart in the chapter. The customized device mentioned in this chapter is meant for agricultural applications. The experimental analysis will be discuss in the coming chapter.

REFERENCES

[1] Casals, L., Mir, B., Vidal, R., & Gomez, C. (2017). Modeling the energy performance of LoRaWAN. *Sensors*, *17*(10), 2364.

[2]   Sinha, R. S., Wei, Y., & Hwang, S. H. (2017). A survey on LPWA technology: LoRa and NB-IoT. *Ict Express*, *3*(1), 14-21.

[3]   Carvalho, D. F., Ferrari, P., Sisinni, E., Depari, A., Rinaldi, S., Pasetti, M., & Silva, D. (2019). A test methodology for evaluating architectural delays of LoRaWAN implementations. *Pervasive and Mobile Computing*.

[4]   Mekki, K., Bajic, E., Chaxel, F., & Meyer, F. (2019). A comparative study of LPWAN technologies for large-scale IoT deployment. *ICT Express*, *5*(1), 1-7.

[5]   Eldefrawy, M., Butun, I., Pereira, N., & Gidlund, M. (2019). Formal security analysis of LoRaWAN. *Computer Networks*, *148*, 328-339.

[6]   https://lora-alliance.org/portals/0/documents/whitepapers/LoRa-Alliance-Whitepaper-LPWA-Technologies.pdf.

[7]   https://www.semtech.com/images/datasheet/an1200.22pdf.

[8]   Marais, J. M., Malekian, R., & Abu-Mahfouz, A. M. (2017, September). LoRa and LoRaWAN testbeds: A review. In *2017 Ieee Africon* (pp. 1496-1501). IEEE.

[9]   de Carvalho Silva, J., Rodrigues, J. J., Alberti, A. M., Solic, P., & Aquino, A. L. (2017, July). LoRaWAN—A low power WAN protocol for Internet of Things: A review and opportunities. In *2017 2nd International Multidisciplinary Conference on Computer and Energy Science (SpliTech)* (pp. 1-6). IEEE.

[10]   Saari, M., bin Baharudin, A. M., Sillberg, P., Hyrynsalmi, S., & Yan, W. (2018, May). LoRa—A survey of recent research trends. In 2018 41st International Convention on Information and Communication Technology, Electronics and Microelectronics (MIPRO) (pp. 0872-0877). IEEE.

[11]   Khutsoane, O., Isong, B., & Abu-Mahfouz, A. M. (2017, October). IoT devices and applications based on LoRa/LoRaWAN. In IECON 2017-43rd Annual Conference of the IEEE Industrial Electronics Society (pp. 6107-6112). IEEE.

[12]   Reda, H. T., Daely, P. T., Kharel, J., & Shin, S. Y. (2018). On the application of IoT: Meteorological information display system based

on LoRa wireless communication. *IETE Technical Review*, *35*(3), 256-265.

[13] Dias, José, and António Grilo. "LoRaWAN multi-hop uplink extension." *Procedia computer science* 130 (2018): 424-431.

[14] El Fehri, C., Kassab, M., Abdellatif, S., Berthou, P., & Belghith, A. (2018). LoRa technology MAC layer operations and Research issues. *Procedia computer science*, *130*, 1096-1101.

[15] Eldefrawy, M., Butun, I., Pereira, N., & Gidlund, M. (2019). Formal security analysis of LoRaWAN. *Computer Networks*, *148*, 328-339.

[16] Casals, L., Mir, B., Vidal, R., & Gomez, C. (2017). Modeling the energy performance of LoRaWAN. *Sensors*, *17*(10), 2364.

[17] Bouguera, T., Diouris, J. F., Chaillout, J. J., Jaouadi, R., & Andrieux, G. (2018). Energy consumption model for sensor nodes based on LoRa and LoRaWAN. *Sensors*, *18*(7), 2104.

[18] Sharma, V., You, I., Pau, G., Collotta, M., Lim, J., & Kim, J. (2018). Lorawan-based energy-efficient surveillance by drones for intelligent transportation systems. *Energies*, 11(3), 573.

[19] Haxhibeqiri, J., De Poorter, E., Moerman, I., & Hoebeke, J. (2018). A survey of lorawan for iot: From technology to application. *Sensors*, 18(11), 3995.

[20] Butun, I., Pereira, N., & Gidlund, M. (2019). Security Risk Analysis of LoRaWAN and Future Directions. *Future Internet*, 11(1), 3.

[21] Vuran, M. C., Salam, A., Wong, R., & Irmak, S. (2018). Internet of underground things in precision agriculture: Architecture and technology aspects. *Ad Hoc Networks*, 81, 160-173.

[22] Ray, P. P. (2017). Internet of things for smart agriculture: Technologies, practices and future direction. *Journal of Ambient Intelligence and Smart Environments*, 9(4), 395-420.

[23] FATHALLAH, K., ABID, M. A., & HADJ-ALOUANE, N. B. Internet of things in the service of precision agriculture.

[24] Ray, P. P. (2018). A survey on Internet of Things architectures. *Journal of King Saud University-Computer and Information Sciences*, 30(3), 291-319.

[25] Ojha, T., Misra, S., & Raghuwanshi, N. S. (2015). Wireless sensor networks for agriculture: The state-of-the-art in practice and future challenges. *Computers and Electronics in Agriculture,* 118, 66-84.

[26] Karim, F., & Karim, F. (2017). Monitoring system using web of things in precision agriculture. *Procedia Computer Science*, 110, 402-409.

[27] Popović, T., Latinović, N., Pešić, A., Zečević, Ž., Krstajić, B., & Djukanović, S. (2017). Architecting an IoT-enabled platform for precision agriculture and ecological monitoring: A case study. *Computers and Electronics in Agriculture,* 140, 255-265.

[28] Tzounis, A., Katsoulas, N., Bartzanas, T., & Kittas, C. (2017). Internet of Things in agriculture, recent advances and future challenges. *Biosystems Engineering*, 164, 31-48.

[29] Botta, A., De Donato, W., Persico, V., & Pescapé, A. (2016). Integration of cloud computing and internet of things: a survey. *Future generation computer systems,* 56, 684-700.

[30] Mekki, K., Bajic, E., Chaxel, F., & Meyer, F. (2019). A comparative study of LPWAN technologies for large-scale IoT deployment. *ICT Express,* 5(1), 1-7.

[31] https://www.microchip.com/wwwproducts/en/ATmega328

In: LoRA and IoT Networks …
Editors: A. Gehlot, R. Singh et al.

ISBN: 978-1-53617-164-8
© 2020 Nova Science Publishers, Inc.

Chapter 3

INDUSTRIAL HAZARD PREVENTION USING XBEE AND IOT

Prabin Kumar Das
Embedded Systems and IoT, Lovely Professional University,
Jalandhar, Punjab, India

ABSTRACT

Industrial hazards are not a very common event that occurs frequently but this rare disaster causes mass damage to human health and wealth whenever it comes into play. Many of our cities are situated very much in contact with various industries and this interaction proves to be a major problem for the people living by in that surrounding. This topic is often very much ignored because of its rare occurrence but we need to give more focus on the development of Hazard prevention measures so that we can predict the disaster earlier and prevent damage to human life as well as natural resources. The main reason for this disaster is the lack of proper care of machinery and unintentionally ignored small faulty lines that in-turn, builds up into large faults and eventually results in an unwanted industrial hazard causing huge damage to human health as well as wealth. In this chapter, we have discussed various technical algorithms comprising of various equipment that will be able to monitor environmental parameters by sensing through different pre-installed nodes deployed at specific positions following a defined algorithm and warn for any undesired changes in those parameters. So it is the validation of a reliable device that can be used to predict as well as prevent hazards to a great extent.

Keywords: Xbee, Raspberry Pi, IoT, Industrial Hazard Prevention, Geiger Counter

INTRODUCTION

Humans of the 21st century always tend to make our lives easier and flexible through various man-made products and resources which promotes the number of industries (e.g., Nuclear power plants, medicinal factories, Gas production lines, etc.) that are very closely connected to people living at every place. If something is very closely connected to us, then it is very obvious to be affected by its every goods and odds. The main component in the list of odds is an Industrial hazard (e.g., Gas leak, Nuclear radiation emission, etc.). Although it is a very rare event and might occur once in a decade, whenever it comes into play it causes mass damage to human health and wealth. Due to its rare practical occurrence, it is often ignored and discussion about its measures for prevention and prediction is very limited which as a result makes people blind handed when an event like this occurs suddenly from nowhere. Proper discussion and implementation of industrial hazard prevention measures can very effectively help in the prediction and prevention of hazard, resulting in a reduced amount of damages.

From a study and analysis of past disasters that have caused maximum damage to human health and wealth one thing in common that was observed for most of them was that the main reason of all these devastating disasters was lack of proper care by staff members and delay in providing alert information to the concerned authorities as well as local civilians. If observed deeply we can notice that at initial stages a disaster is basically a mere mistake or fault in the machinery, which when not detected or taken proper care eventually grows up into devastating disaster, there is a scope that if we can detect the fault earlier, we can effectively prevent the disaster.

Disaster planning methods and immediate response during a disaster cannot be achieved by any simple technique or algorithm, it requires complex and more scientific analysis for an effective action plan. The phases of the detection and rescue process need a highly efficient mechanism, which should be able to predict the disaster, prevent up to considerable level and trigger immediate assistance during an emergency. In this chapter, we focus on designing nodes powered by solar energy rechargeable cells with pre-installed various environmental parameter sensing sensors that are to be deployed inside an industry at specified positions following a zonal mapping and as well as in its nearby areas surrounding it for further data analysis.

REVIEW OF LITERATURE

Disaster Prevention or prediction cannot be achieved through basic mechanisms implementation, it needs a very highly specific scientific and analytical approach for its proper and precise implementation of prevention and emergency trigger algorithms. This needs the data acquired for analysis to be very précised, having no delay so that any unwanted situations can be detected, analyzed and further countered. [1] Every field of study related to disasters nowadays only focused on the analysis of the disaster rather than focusing on its prevention and prediction mechanisms. We know that analysis of previous disasters can reduce the number of disasters to some extent but will never be able to prevent it in any way. This paper focuses on all-around aspects of a disaster comprising of disaster planning, training, response as well as relief methodologies. [2] This paper is basically focused on the most commonly used as well as very inflammable gas LPG. This uses some sensors to monitor the level of LPG and also during any event of leakage it sends an alert signal to the user through a GSM module instantly. [3] This system proposal focuses on the detection and immediate emergency triggering for any event of gas leakage like (LPG, isobutene, cigarette smoke, etc.) in case of any leakage event its output goes low and it is considered as an event of leakage. Instantly an alert message through the GSM module is sent to the user and exhaust are turned on after a delay of few milliseconds. [4] This proposal includes a mechanism for radiation detection. In case of any event of radiation leakage, the device mechanism uses any proximate mobile personal communication for sending an alert message to the authorities and as well as it predicts the possible source of radiation nearby. This basically aims to create a device included inside mobile communication for radiation detection without any human interference. [5] This proposed mechanism aims to present a device using GPS and other radiation sensors to detect the radiation leakage and provide alert information about the real-time value of the radiation level along with its location to the user through a wireless zig Bee communication protocol. It has been proposed to support both the continuous and intermittent modes of measurement to make it more reliable and effective. [6] In this proposal, targeting construction industrial hazards and accidents a fuzzy risk assessment method has been countered. Various methods have been implemented to analyze various types of hazards and their root causes. To assess the risk of hazards, FMEA (Failure modes and effect analysis) has been performed based on the last conclusions and the reasoning of the previous data based on the fuzzy inference approach. [7] In this paper various contributing factors like fall size, company size and individual factors like age, gender, experience has been studied and graphed for analyzing the major causes of accidents. Primary measures like fixed barriers, strong handrails and secondary type measures like travel restraint systems (safety belt), fall arrest systems were proposed to prevent or reduce the consequences of these accidents. [8] In this paper the hazards in chemical industries of Korea due to fire, explosion or release of harmful gases have been targeted particularly as a critical issue. A PCM system was introduced and implemented in every industry under which the business owner of such places shall submit a safety report consisting of various information regarding the level of safety measures implemented inside the industry to the government to prevent accidents which can inflict an immediate damage to health as well as wealth in the vicinity of the workplaces or industry [9] This idea mainly focuses on the linkage of different factors with simple and accurate strategies. The aim of the current work is to explicitly link the inherent safety principles of minimization, substitution, moderation, and simplification with strategies for dust explosion prevention and mitigation. Various discussions were performed for implementing various ways to minimize, substitute, moderate and simplify dust hazards. Particular attention is paid to the relationship between each inherent safety principle, various dust explosibility parameters, alternate methods of processing, selection of process equipment, development and implementation of safe-work procedures [10] For air quality monitoring the Air Quality Index (AQI) is important. It is an index prepared by government institutions to categories the risk of air pollution. Lower AQI value represents pleasant air quality. Stated is the AQI index value adopted by India. The various algorithm and hardware descriptions to read the various gas sensors for monitor and control applications. [11, 12, 13] The main aim of this study is to deal with the industrial accident and the effect that an industrial accident prevails thereafter in the industrial plant and its vicinity. It has been said that the interaction and behavior of past accidents or we can say old targets that have affected previously can be studied and analyzed to prepare measures or predict in a certain condition and as a result reduce the impact on new targets very effectively to a great extent. The initial sequence is maybe generating some set of information about the risks due to the blast wave and another factor on the time of the first hazard. [14] In this paper, one of the many harmful substances that can cause mass damage to human health and wealth and also very widely used in the industrial sector is targeted, which is Beryllium exposure. It has been depicted that the workers working in the sector who are exposed to this harmful substance suffer from many acute and chronic problems related to health. The most dangerous ill effect of this is causing dangerous lung disease because they develop a lymphocyte-mediated sensitization to the metal which is completely unnatural and is very harmful to any human body's wellbeing. All the workers working in various industrial sectors/fields like nuclear, aerospace, telecommunication, electronics, biomedical and semiconductor industries are at severe risk to their physical and mental state of well-being. So many public health actions like the study of the bioavailability of different physicochemical forms of beryllium, skin protection in preventing sensitization in high risk are discussed and planned for implementation for the prevention of disease. [15]

In this paper basically a crucial problem that is common in most of the industry has been discussed, which is lifting heavy weights by the workers or employees during their job which gradually becomes the main reason for back injuries. An accident prevention education system was specially designed to eliminate or reduce the causes of back injuries up to a significant level. In this paper, it was clearly mentioned that there is no specific way or procedure for lifting loads or weights in the industry. It was also mentioned in this paper that postural fatigue in case of back injury is often neglected in the inquiries. [16] Carbon tetrachloride was used as an anesthetic in place of chloroform, but it was very harmful because it is found having high chlorine content and most frequent commercial use of carbon tetrachloride is as a solvent in rubber, chemical, drug and paint industry, cleansing agent in the dry cleaning industry, and anthelmintic for parasites in practice of medicine. [17] In this paper they have basically aimed towards conducting a study to examine the nature and scope of dust explosion risks in the industry and to identify initiatives that may be very much helpful and effective for the prevention of combustible dust fires and explosions. It was mentioned that such initiatives may include regulatory action, voluntary consensus standards, or other measures that must be regularly and carefully implemented by people of various levels. This study also includes the study and thorough analysis of past incidents to predict or have an idea about the severity level of the problem that may occur in present or near future. [18] In this paper the harmful effects of "nitrous fume" have been taken into consideration for discussion. The main attention in this particular paper has been drawn to the fact of inhaling the harmful "nitrous fume". The study of nitrous fume in the case of Britain from the last ten years are also shown in the paper along with a recent environmental survey conducted in the shipyard and repair yard along the northeast coast of England. [19] In this proposal of a system, the development of an environmental screening program to analyze the effect of chemicals which have a potential risk to human health is very carefully studied and discussed. In this proposal, all the data which is publicly available have been extracted into Aggregated Computational Toxicology Resource which combines the information for several chemicals from public sources. [20] This paper is basically focused on industrial noise hazards. The proposed mechanism along with the study shows that some of the industries which are associated with continuous exposure to loud noise, lead to temporary or even permanent deafness to its workers, because of its innocuous from the high-frequency range sounds. It is claimed that the number of affected workers is multiplying because of the increased production of tools such as a pneumatically operated hammer, chipper and a riveting gun in very confined areas. [21] In this paper they have basically aimed for designing a feedback package system that is used to prevent the occupational accidents which directly fit into the normal operation of any industry. For this proposal, eighteen different hazardous conditions were first thoroughly studied and depending upon those hazardous conditions, a counter feedback package was presented in different forms correspondingly. By this, it was observed that the frequency of hazards was drastically dropped by up to 60%. After that, a modified feedback system was designed and implemented according to the needs of the specific industries. [22] This proposal of a system focuses on static electricity as a potential ignition risk in different industrial operations. As a counter to this problem, observation on the basis of data being used in the industries is being used to develop safety processes for the industry and several other problems are taken into consideration for modification and up-gradation in safety measures and thereby developing an effective solution for this problem. [23] In this paper they have basically aimed at the implementation and promotion of industrial waste reuse procedures which in their opinion has resulted in the reduction of pollution in Taiwan. In order to use and handle natural resources safely for their benefits and growth, Taiwan's Environmental Protection Administration (EPA), which is in cooperation with the Ministry of Economic Affairs (MOEA), has discussed the promotional programs for the reuse of waste materials that are produced in a very large scale in industries and by its implementation they expected a lot more reduction in pollution that was caused due to dumping or sinking of industrial wastage. [24] The main aim of this study is to deal with fire hazards in the industrial sector. In this paper, a new safety device was proposed to monitor the process of cooking for various parameters, mainly temperature that is to be done by live temperature sensing sensors. The safety device is planned to be customized according to the need and type of the industry and by taking into consideration the actual temperature as a reference value. [25] This paper is basically focused on the moral hazards between different countries of Asia. Moral hazards are mainly caused due to overprotecting industrial policies. To prevent moral hazards, the government also guarantees depending on the industrial firms and it is also determined or bounded to discuss the moral hazard arguments in the presence of the International Monetary Fund (IMF). [26] The main aim of the study is to deal with the major hazard sources identification in the iron and steel production industry. As the working and manufacturing process of metals like iron is complex and there is a lot of raw material usage during its preparation. To reduce the chance of any industrial accident it is very important to identify the source or root cause of the hazard. This present study provides data by analyzing various databases based on characteristics and property of the materials used for manufacturing, which concludes that the risk source or major hazard sources are completely based on the characteristics and quality of the hazardous substance that is being used in production lines of industries. [27] In this paper they have basically aimed at the hazards caused due to human- mimic and human-collaborative industrial robots that are used for different industrial applications. The analysis is then applied to a new industrial upper body humanoid which is under development and the result of the analysis is processed by Fishbone diagram analysis for further study and implementation work. [28] This study has basically focused on a very basic chemical element named Hydrogen peroxide that is very rapidly and widely used in many industries as a reagent. The study of the butadiene free radical with hydrogen peroxide was conducted in the presence of an organic solvent and the data acquired from that experiment is analyzed with the main aim for studying the influence of impurities on heat reactions. [29]

DIAGRAMS

1. Zonal Mapping

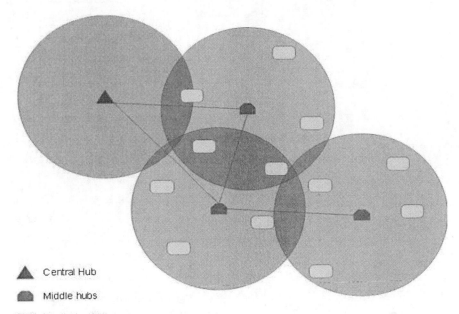

Central Hub

Middle hubs

Monitoring Hubs

Figure 1. Zonal Mapping.

Above Figure 1 shows the zonal mapping of the nodes and their connections for sending and receiving real-time data values. In this stand-alone nodes are deployed at specific positions following the zonal mapping inside the specific industry. These end nodes are connected to the middle hub, which then sends data to the final main node situated at the control room for further analysis and logging into the server for implementation.

Prabin Kumar Das

2. End Node

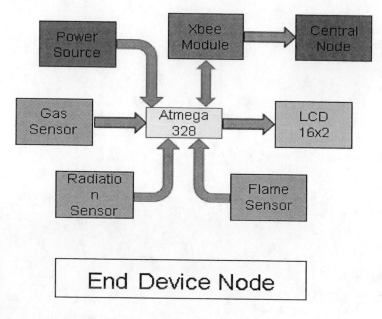

Figure 2. End Node.

Above Figure 2 shows a block diagram of the components connected to the end node. Sensors that are used depends upon the type of industry and the parameters we are focusing on and which can cause a hazard. These sensors work by reading the environmental parameters in real-time and send them for analysis to the main node using a ZigBee module that is acting as a transmitter for real-time data exchange. The microcontroller that is connected to the central hub having a ZigBee module which is acting there as a receiver for data sharing and further analysis of data.

3. Central Node

Below Figure 3 shows the block diagrams of components that are present in a main central node. The main node having an Xbee module acting as a data receiver in real-time receives the data from all the end nodes and processes them according to the predefined algorithm and comparing the values to the set max threshold and decides the condition as a normal or abnormal proximity condition. It simultaneously logs the real-time status into the dedicated server for further analysis and implementation through any way of internet connectivity such as Ethernet or GPRS module.

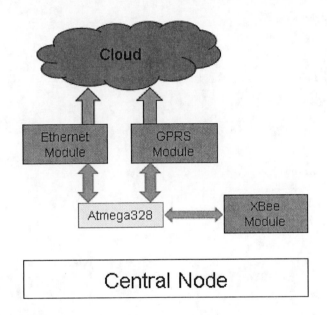

Figure 3. Main Central Node.

4. Raspberry Pi

The Raspberry Pi is a tiny and affordable computer that can be used to learn to program. It was originally intended to help spur interest in computing among small school-aged children but other than this as well it has many other applications in the field of computing and also for the customization of various stand-alone devices that needs a compact but powerful microcomputer for their implementation. This runs totally on open-source software which makes it very much compatible to be interfaced with any kind of device and to be used for various applications without any such limits effectively and efficiently.

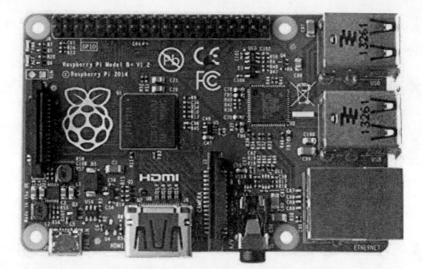

Figure 4. Raspberry Pi.

5. Arduino UNO R3

Figure 5. Arduino UNO.

The Arduino UNO is a removable Dual Inline Package (DIP) ATmega328 AVR based easily programmable microcontroller having 20 digital I/O pins (i.e., 6 are assigned as PWM digital output pins, 6 are normal digital output pins and 6 are used as analog input pins). It is a very effective and user-friendly microcontroller very widely used by beginners for getting aquatinted with the basics of microprocessors and microcontrollers. The R3 is the third and latest version of the basic Arduino UNO. It's a very reliable and easy to use a microcontroller for various IoT applications in a different field. Its wide compatibility makes it more reliable because the user can modify and re-modify the peripheral devices according to his/her will at any point in working which makes it more easy for re-modification.

6. Nuttify

Figure 6. Nuttify.

Nuttify is an Internet of Things Hardware platform based on the ESP8266 12e series that enables the user to build IoT products, Research Analysis Systems, Automation, and Projects. Using Nuttify, users can monitor, manage, control and search devices from any part of the world. It's can also interface with any IoT web servers, iCloud, Local or IOT mobile platform or application easily. A number of services open source web servers & mobile apps are available on the internet that is freeware to use. It can prove very effective and useful for any user who wants to use Wi-Fi as its network connectivity source. Due to its hard built and compact hardware, it is also very reliable for most of the applications.

7. Xbee Module

Figure 7. ZigBee Module.

ZigBee is an IEEE 802.15.4-based specification for a suite of high-level communication protocols used to create personal area networks with small, low-power digital radios, such as for home automation, medical device data collection, and other low-power low-bandwidth needs, designed for small scale projects which need wireless connection. Hence, ZigBee is a low-power, low data rate, and close proximity (i.e., personal area) wireless ad hoc network. This is very suitable for implementation in an industrial area. It is a form of RF communication that works with the usage of Direct Sequence *Spread Spectrum* (DSSS).

In the 2.4 GHz band, a maximum over-the-air data rate of 250 kbps is specified, but due to the overhead of the protocol, the actual theoretical maximum data rate is approximately half of that.

8. Geiger Counter

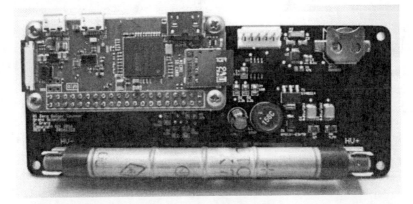

Figure 8. Geiger counter.

A Geiger counter is an instrument used for detecting and measuring ionizing radiation. Also known as a Geiger-Mueller counter (or Geiger-Müller counter), it is widely used in applications such as radiation dosimetry, radiological protection, experimental physics, and the nuclear industry. This device works with the principle of using the ionization effect that is artificially produced in a Geiger–Müller tube which detects any contact rays of ionizing radiations including alpha, beta, and gamma rays.

9. MQ Gas Sensor

Figure 9. MQ Gas sensor.

The MQ series of gas sensors use a small heater inside with an electrochemical sensor. They are sensitive for a range of gasses and are used for sensing various gas parameters. This gives an analog output that can be given to a microcontroller for an effective analysis. The accuracy and reliability of these sensors depend on the quality that is being used in it.

10. Flame Sensor

Figure 10. Flame Sensor.

These sensors work with the principle of UV radiation detections. It detects the UV radiation emitted from the event of ignition events and often creates a 2-3 seconds delay to prevent a false alarm.

11. Buzzer

Figure 11. Buzzer.

A buzzer or beeper is a device basically used for alert or alarming applications These are of different types according to their field of application i.e., mechanical, electromechanical or piezoelectric types.

CIRCUIT DIAGRAMS

Below Figure 12 shows the circuits and connections of all the equipment used in this device implementation. It consists of circuitry details of main microcontroller Raspberry Pi, Arduino, Xbee module, MQ2 gas sensor, Geiger counter, and buzzer.

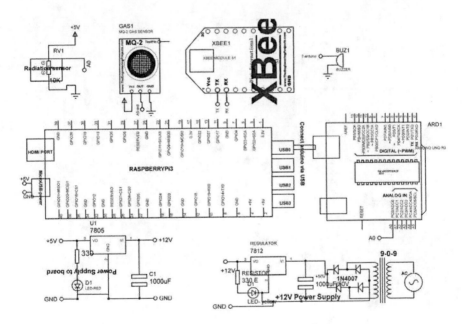

Figure 12. Circuit Details.

Once deployed at specific positions, the microcontroller starts taking values of the targeted environmental parameters through sensors connected to it and sends them through a connected ZigBee module acting as a transmitter in real-time to the central or main node. Once the data values are received by the central node through a ZigBee module acting as a receiver, it analyses the data and specifies them as at a normal safe level or as a proximity event according to the set max threshold. it also logs all the status into a dedicated server for further analyses and implementation. For interfacing with analog output sensors, we have used ARDUINO because there is no provision of analog pins input on Raspberry Pi. We have implemented Pyfirmeta protocol to create a gateway for interaction between Arduino and Raspberry Pi.

END NODE

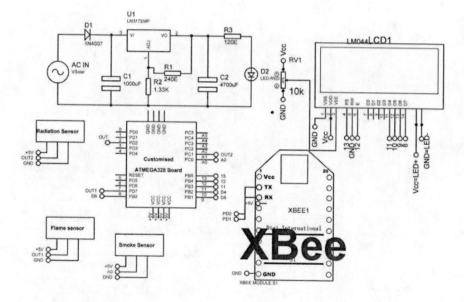

Figure 13. End Node.

Above Figure 13 depicts the circuit description of the components of a sample end node that consists of a power supply, a linear voltage regulator, a 16*2 LCD, a Customized Atmega 328 based microcontroller board, a MQ series gas sensor, an IR based flame sensor, a radiation sensor (i.e., Geiger counter) and a Xbee module. Here, during its active state of operation of the end node the Customized Atmega 328 based microcontroller board will get the values of the real-time levels of the environmental parameters (here gas, radiation and flame) by using the connected sensors, display it on the LCD display and send them to the central node for further analysis and implementation by using a Xbee module connected to it which acts as a data transmitter in real-time manner.

CENTRAL NODE USING NUTTYFI

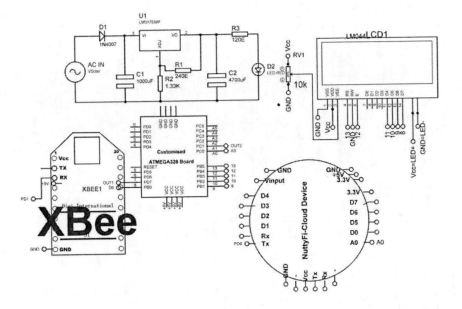

Figure 14. Central Node using Nuttify.

Above Figure 14 depicts the circuit description of the components of a sample Central node using Nuttify that consists of a power supply, a linear voltage regulator, a 16*2 LCD, a customized Atmega 328 based microcontroller board, an Xbee module, and a Nuttify. This type of sample central node receives the data consisting of the values of environmental parameters from the various end nodes in real-time with the help of a connected Xbee module acting as a receiver and simultaneously logs the values of the environmental parameters as well as the status of each end node's zone as normal/safe or abnormal/unsafe into the server by using Nuttify. Nuttify is basically a customized Atmega 328 based microcontroller board having a Wi-Fi module inbuilt in it which thereby allows the user to easily access/interface internet with their devices using Wi-Fi connectivity very reliably.

CENTRAL NODE USING RASPBERRY PI

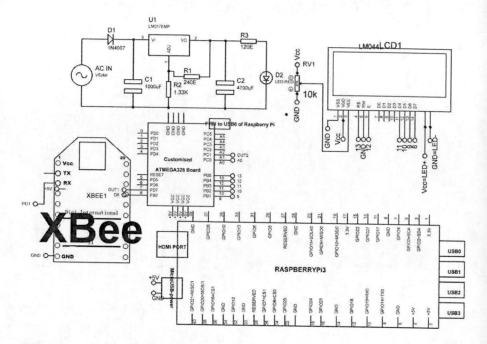

Figure 15. Central Node using Raspberry Pi.

Above Figure 15 depicts the circuit description of the components of a sample Central node using Nuttify that consists of a power supply, a linear voltage regulator, a 16*2 LCD, a customized Atmega 328 based microcontroller board, an Xbee module and a Raspberry Pi. This type of central node works by receiving the data consisting of the values of the environmental parameters by using an Xbee module acting as a receiver in real-time. After analysis by comparison of the data with the set max threshold value of each parameter, it states the status of the end nodes zones as in safe or unsafe conditions. It simultaneously logs the values received and the status of the end node into the dedicated server for further analysis and implementation. Here, the purpose of especially using Raspberry Pi is because to interface a server and log sensitive data we need continuous internet connectivity and it might happen that at some place the option of Wi-Fi connectivity might not be available or not properly functioning. So, to eliminate this problem an Ethernet cable connection can be easily used with Raspberry Pi port to provide continuous and fast internet connectivity for server applications in real-time and emergency triggers during a proximity event.

SOFTWARE DEVELOPMENT

Once the device is deployed at the targeted zone and provided with required power supply it is set to ON state and immediately it configures itself to sense the real-time values of the environmental parameters through the attached sensors on it (sensors attached may vary according to the specific target area or industry). The data sensed is then send to the main node from the end node using the ZigBee module without any delay in the form of discrete packets. Microcontroller attached with a ZigBee receiver at the main node receives the data and compares the values with the max set threshold values. If after analysis the values seem to be normal then it logs the values into server and the same process repeats, otherwise if after analysis the values seem to be higher than normal or increasing abruptly the condition is treated as a proximity condition by the programmed microcontroller and it immediately triggers an alert information consisting of the exact zone's location having the abnormal level and the parameter that is increasing to the concerned authorities through the dedicated server and activates all emergency action that is pre-specified through various actuators.. The process is depicted in the form of a flow chart in Figure 16 below.

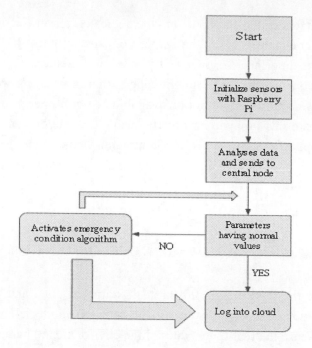

Figure 16. Flow Chart.

CODES

- Burn the below code through Arduino IDE for main node (receiving end)

------------------------------"START FROM HERE" ------------------------------

```
#include <ESP8266HTTPClient.h>
#include <ESP8266WiFi.h>
String api_key = "API KEY";
String toggle_id = "ENTER_TOGGLE_WIDGET_ID";
String text_id = "TEXT ID";

int t, h;
void setup()
```

```
{
  Serial.begin(9600);
  WiFi.begin("SSID", "PASSWORD");        //Setup for connection to
Wi-Fi
  Serial.println("Waiting for connection");
   while (WiFi.status() != WL_CONNECTED)
    {                                      //Used until successful
connection to Wi-Fi
       delay(500);
       Serial.println(".");
    }
}
void loop()
{
  if (WiFi.status() == WL_CONNECTED) {
    if (Serial.available()<1)
    return;
   String R=Serial.readString();
   Serial.println(getValue(R,':', 0));
   Serial.println(getValue(R,':', 1));
   Serial.println(postText("be9b732f8ae1498b", getValue(R,':', 0)));
   Serial.println(postText("c1ae00b5b30ca7a0", getValue(R,':', 1)));
   if (getValue(R,':', 0).toInt() > 50 || getValue(R,':', 2).toInt() > 5) {
      Serial.println(postText("4ad3589baf81bff1", "Unsafe"));
      digitalWrite(D7,HIGH);
    } else {
     Serial.println(postText("4ad3589baf81bff1", "Safe"));
    }
  }
}
String postText(String text_id, String text_value)
{
   HTTPClient http;
```

```
http.begin("http://api.iotsardar.com/v1/user/post/text");          //setting
    up destination for request
http.addHeader("Content-Type",                    "application/x-www-form-
    urlencoded"); //Specifying content-type header
  int httpCode = http.POST("api_key=" + api_key + "&text_id=" +
    text_id + "&text_value=" + text_value); //Sending request
  if (httpCode == 200)
  {                              // code 200 means data received successfully
      String textReturn = http.getString(); //Get the request response
payload
      return textReturn;
  }
  else
  {
    String textReturn = "error"; // return error
    Serial.println(httpCode);
    return textReturn;
  }
  http.end(); //Close connection
}
String getValue(String data, char separator, int index) {
  int found = 0;
  int strIndex[] = {0, -1};
  int maxIndex = data.length()-1;
  for(int i=0; i<=maxIndex && found<=index; i++){
  if(data.charAt(i)==separator || i==maxIndex){
    found++;
    strIndex[0] = strIndex[1]+1;
    strIndex[1] = (i == maxIndex) ? i+1 : i;
  }
  }
  return found>index ? data.substring(strIndex[0], strIndex[1]) : "";
}
```

- Burn the below code through Arduino IDE for END node (transmitting end)

----------------------------"START FROM HERE" -----------------------
----

```
//This code is capable of reading temperature and humidity through a
    DHT sensor, LPG through MQ sensor and detect fire through an IR
    sensor.
#include <DHT.h>
#include <SoftwareSerial.h>
SoftwareSerial mySerial(6, 7);
 #define DHTPIN 2

// Uncomment the type of sensor in use:
 #define DHTTYPE DHT11
int ir_val;
DHT_Unified dht(DHTPIN, DHTTYPE);

float mqVoltage;
float mqValue;
void setup()
 {
    digitalWrite(10,LOW);
    digitalWrite(11,HIGH);
    int ir_val=digitalRead(4);
    pinMode(3,INPUT);
    pinMode(4,INPUT);
    Serial.begin(9600);
    mySerial.begin(9600);
  }
 void loop()
 {
    // Get Sensor data
    sensors_event_t tempEvent;
```

```
sensors_event_t humEvent;
dht.temperature().getEvent(&tempEvent);
dht.humidity().getEvent(&humEvent);
for(int i = 0; i < 100; i++){
  mqValue = mqValue + analogRead(0); // read analog input pin 0
}
mqValue = mqValue / 100;              // Getting the
average from the values
mqVoltage = mqValue/1024*5.0;          //converting the
values into voltage
    mySerial.print(ir_val);
    mySerial.print(":");
    mySerial.println(mqVoltage);
    Serial.println(mqVoltage);
    Serial.print(":");
    Serial.print(ir_val);
  delay(2000);
}
```

RESULTS AND DISCUSSION

In curiosity of knowing the level of effectiveness and reliability of this proposed device at various practical proximity and hazard conditions a basic prototype of this device has been designed and developed by targeting a LPG gas industry which works for storing the various types of flammable gases.

Sensors like MQ2, IR, DHT has been used during the testing of this device for specific purpose of MQ for measuring the LPG gas level in the atmosphere and giving a change in voltage as output for exact value calculation, IR sensor for detecting the emerging of fire by using the infrared waves falling into the photosensitive diode present in the sensor that a fire splits out during explosion, DHT sensor for getting the information about the present temperature and humidity of the target place which can be used for prediction of an abrupt rise in temperature or abnormal change in humidity of the industry target place. Although various other sensors depending upon the type of target industry can be used with the device like Geiger counter for effective calculation of rising in radiation level in the nuclear industry, other MQ series sensor for sensing another type of gases that may lead to a hazard in industries like pesticide storage (*Bhopal Gas Plant*).

During testing of this prototype, it gave a very positive result in detecting the faults and fulfilling the ambition with significant precision. Nodes connected with the sensors and microcontrollers were firstly deployed at a place resembling the proximity condition and made to be inactive mode by supplying power supply. It showed effective sensing of real-time environmental parameters through the microcontroller and the values received at the main node end were also without any delay. A Raspberry Pi was used at the main end node for receiving the values from the end node through a ZigBee module receiver because an Ethernet connection can be used with Raspberry Pi for uninterrupted logging into the server.

According to predefined algorithm whenever it received an abrupt or abnormal rise in any environmental parameters more than a set max threshold, it takes this event as a proximity condition for hazard and instantly activates its alarm features through the buzzer and also sends an alert warning along with the location of observed abrupt rise and parameter that is rising onto the server instantly as well as to the concerned authorities.

Figure 17 depicts the snapshots of the proposed device's prototype that consist of an End node (1st picture from right) designed to be deployed at specific positions to sense real-time values of the environmental parameters and send them to the main node (middle picture) through Xbee module for further analysis and actions.

Figure 18 shows the snapshot of the interface of the customized server (IOT SARDAR) that was effectively used during the prototype testing of the proposed device. It shows the real-time values of the LPG level and temperature of the targeted zone/area. After reading the data and analysis it is also depicting the real-time condition as in safe zone or should be taken

as a proximity condition through that status toggle button present at the top
of the screen board.

Figure 17. View of the system.

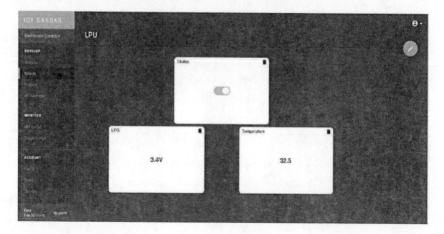

Figure 18. Server records.

CONCLUSION

Planning for prediction of a disaster and its prevention cannot be achieved with any simple approach or algorithm. It requires a high-end analysis and scientific approach. Mapping or dividing the target industry into zones for deciding the position of nodes deployment and the configuration of their sensors are the main advantage of this proposal. This allows us with very highly précised detection of the fault line area because the abnormal rise in the environmental parameters will be observed first in the node that is present nearby it and as we have deployed nodes with specific zone, we can have an idea of the zonal area having that specific node. This will help us to minimize the delay in detection and as a result safety measures can be taken immediately for preventing the fault from further getting more devastating.

For the further need of sensing various analog sensors, Arduino along with raspberry pi can be used with the pyfirmeta protocol as a gateway for the same. In the case of the Main node, the purpose of using raspberry pi is due to the need for proper continuous internet connectivity which can be easily provided by an Ethernet connection through Raspberry Pi. It is taken with much consideration because in the case where we are dealing with sensitive readings of the sensors in real-time, it is very much required that the data and the status should be updated to the server in real-time without any delay because there is no scope of mistake in analysis of such data which when goes wrong can result in huge damage to human health as well as wealth.

This system also has a scope of improvement for extending its effectiveness, which can be achieved by implementing various aspects of Machine Learning and Artificial Intelligence by which a neural network may be trained by using any learning technique by providing the daily values of the sensors and corresponding status of the condition/event (i.e., safe/unsafe) in an industry for some specific period of time and then that learned neural network can be used and implemented to analyze a given random data set comprising of sensor values during any day to predict the possibility of a hazard by calculating the changes from past experience of conditions having similar data values like the provided data set. It will definitely increase the device's capability of précised decision making and even emergency help provision capability up to a great extent without or negligible human interference in its mechanism.

Natural disasters are such events that cannot be eliminated by human force but their devasting effect upon human health and wealth also cannot be ignored. This present proposal of our device in this chapter can be effectively used for early prediction, instant warning facility and as well as for reliable real-time monitoring of industrial hazard-prone areas all over the globe. Due to the implementation of data logging into the cloud it enables the data acquisition and analysis at any point, as a result, it makes the system effective, efficient as well as very reliable. As an add-on, by using the logged data from the server we can monitor the effects of any industry upon its surroundings and can further advise or order them to improve or change their working procedures and machinery.

REFERENCES

[1]   David Alexander, Book Name: *"Disaster and Emergency Planning for Preparedness, Response, and Recovery."* Subject: Recovery, Risk Management, Response, Preparedness Online Publication Date: Sep 2015.

[2]   Michele Masellis, Springer Books Book Name: *"Thermal agent disaster and fire disaster: definition, damage, assessment and relief operations,"* 978-0-585-33973-3.

[3]   AnkitSood, Babalusonkar, AtulRajan and Mr. Ameer Faisal, "Micro controller based LPG weighing and detector using GSM module." *International Journal of Electrical and Electronics Research* Vol. 3, Issue 2, pp: (264-269), Month: April-June 2015.

[4]   Tanvira Ismail, Devoleena Das, JyotirmoySaikai, JyotirmoyDeka and Rajkumar Sharma. "GSM based gas leakage warning system." *IJARCCE4C* 2278-1021 Vol. 3, Issue 4, April 2014.

[5] Balchunas, Curt, and David Rogers. *"Radiation detection and tracking with GPS-enabled wireless communication system."* U.S. Patent Application 10/795,659, filed May 11, 2006.

[6] Ding, Fei, Guangming Song, Kaijian Yin, Jianqing Li, and Aiguo Song. "A GPS-enabled wireless sensor network for monitoring radioactive materials." *Sensors and Actuators A: Physical 155,* no. 1 (2009): 210-215.

[7] Liu, Hao-Tien, and Yieh-lin Tsai. "A fuzzy risk assessment approach for occupational hazards in the construction industry." *Safety science* 50, no. 4 (2012): 1067-1078.

[8] Chi, Chia-Fen, Tin-Chang Chang, and Hsin-I. Ting. "Accident patterns and prevention measures for fatal occupational falls in the construction industry." *Applied ergonomics* 36, no. 4 (2005): 391-400.

[9] Kwon, Hyuck-myun. "The effectiveness of process safety management (PSM) regulation for chemical industry in Korea." *Journal of Loss Prevention in the Process Industries* 19, no. 1 (2006): 13-16.

[10] Amyotte, Paul R., Michael J. Pegg, and Faisal I. Khan. "Application of inherent safety principles to dust explosion prevention and mitigation." *Process Safety and Environmental Protection* 87, no. 1 (2009): 35-39.

[11] Rajesh Singh, Rohit Samkaria, Anita Gehlot, Neeraj Kumar, Kausal Rawat, Aisik De, AdilRehman, "Algorithm to read various sensors to detect the hazardous parameters in industry", *International Journal of Engineering and Technology* (UAE), 7.2 (2018) (Scopus Indexed).

[12] Anita Gehlot, Rajesh Singh, Rohit Samkaria, Sushabhan Choudhury, Aisik De, Kamlesh, "Air quality and water quality monitoring using Xbee and internet of things." *International Journal of Engineering and Technology (UAE),* 7.2 (2018) (Scopus Indexed).

[13] Neeraj Kumar Singh, Amardeep Singh, Rajesh Singh, Anita Gehlot, "Design and development of air quality management devices with sensors and web of things." *International Journal of Engineering and Technology (UAE),* 7.2 (2018). (Scopus Indexed)

[14] Ahmed, Mebarki, Sandra Jerez, Igor Matasic, Gaëtan Prodhomme, and Mathieu Reimeringer. "Explosions and structural fragments as industrial hazard: domino effect and risks." *Procedia Engineering* 45 (2012): 159-166.

[15] Kreiss, Kathleen, Gregory A. Day, and Christine R. Schuler. "Beryllium: a modern industrial hazard." *Annu. Rev. Public Health* 28 (2007): 259-277.

[16] Brown, John R. "Lifting as an industrial hazard." *American Industrial Hygiene Association Journal* 34, no. 7 (1973): 292-297.

[17] Davis, Paul A. "Carbon tetrachloride as an industrial hazard." *Journal of the American Medical Association* 103, no. 13 (1934): 962-966.

[18] Joseph, Giby, and CSB Hazard Investigation Team. "Combustible dusts: A serious industrial hazard." *Journal of hazardous materials* 142, no. 3 (2007): 589-591.

[19] Morley, R., and S. J. Silk. "The industrial hazard from nitrous fumes." *Annals of Occupational Hygiene* 13, no. 2 (1970): 101-107.

[20] Egeghy, Peter P., Richard Judson, Sumit Gangwal, Shad Mosher, Doris Smith, James Vail, and Elaine A. Cohen Hubal. "The exposure data landscape for manufactured chemicals." *Science of the Total Environment* 414 (2012): 159-166.

[21] McCoy, David A. "The industrial noise hazard." *Archives of Otolaryngology* 39, no. 4 (1944): 327-330.

[22] Sulzer-Azaroff, Beth, and M. Consuelo de Santamaria. "Industrial safety hazard reduction through performance feedback." *Journal of applied behavior analysis* 13, no. 2 (1980): 287-295.

[23] Gibson, Norbert. "Static electricity—an industrial hazard under control?." *Journal of electrostatics* 40 (1997): 21-30.

[24] Tsai, W. T., and Y. H. Chou. "Government policies for encouraging industrial waste reuse and pollution prevention in Taiwan." *Journal of Cleaner Production* 12, no. 7 (2004): 725-736.

[25] Urban, Bezalel, and David Weisman. "Fire hazard prevention system." U.S. Patent Application 10/492,511, filed December 2, 2004.

[26] Chang, Ha-Joon. "The hazard of moral hazard: untangling the Asian crisis." *World development* 28, no. 4 (2000): 775-788.

[27] Chunli, Zhao, and Liu Tiantian Du Juan. "Major Environmental Hazard Source Identification in Iron & Steel Enterprises [J]." *Environmental Science and Management* 4 (2012).

[28] Ogure, Takuya, Yoshihiro Nakabo, SeongHee Jeong, and Yoji Yamada. "Hazard analysis of an industrial upper-body humanoid." *Industrial Robot: An International Journal* 36, no. 5 (2009): 469-476.

[29] De Filippis, P., C. Giavarini, and R. Silla. "Thermal hazard in a batch process involving hydrogen peroxide." *Journal of Loss Prevention in the Process Industries* 15, no. 6 (2002): 449-453.

In: LoRA and IoT Networks …   ISBN: 978-1-53617-164-8
Editors: A. Gehlot, R. Singh et al.   © 2020 Nova Science Publishers, Inc.

Chapter 4

ESSENTIAL ASPECTS OF DAY TO DAY LIFE AND ITS INFLUENCE ON INDUSTRY 4.0

P. S. Ranjit[1,] and Amit Kumar Thakur[2]*
[1]Aditya Engineering College(A), Surampalem, Andhra Pradesh, India
[2]Lovely Professional University, Punjab, India

ABSTRACT

Some of the vital elements that play an important role in our day to day life are food, power, and transport. These are regarded as major factors of human existence. Based on this perspective, the chapter deals with significant sustainable elements of smart agriculture, lighting, and parking. Firstly, smart agriculture is a methodology for altering and reorienting rural generation frameworks and food value chains to promote and ensure the safety of sustenance in the context of environmental change. Secondly, lighting incorporates the use of both counterfeit light sources, such as lights and lighting devices, just as standard lighting is done by sunlight. The central theme of the chapter deals with smart parking. Finding a parking space for drivers to park their vehicles has always ended up with the disillusioning problem. Identifying an appropriate parking space has been troublesome factor for drivers since it creates a heavy traffic jam at the

---
* Corresponding Author's Email: psranjit1234@gmail.com.

global level. In this respect, this chapter deals with intelligent agriculture, with the emphasis on food security, the effects of environmental change on agribusiness, lighting, and intelligent parking aspects.

Keywords: agriculture, lighting, and parking

SMART AGRICULTURE

It is estimated that by 2050, the entire population of the world will increase by 33 percent. The vast majority of these additional 2 billion people live with high dense areas. On the other hand, the Food and Agriculture Organization (FAO) of the United Nations assesses that economic creation should increase by 60% by 2050 to meet standard demands for food and feed [1]. Farming must, in this manner, alter itself to promotes the growth of the world's population and give rise to financial growth and destitution.

Environmental change renders this task more and more difficult in the current scenario, due to antagonistic impacts on agriculture, requiring spiraling adjustment and related costs. To achieve the goals of food safety and agricultural improvement, adjustments to environmental variations and lower discharge powers per output are essential. This shift must be made without the ordinary asset base being exhausted. Environmental variation is the effect of agribusiness and sustenance safety as a result of the increased commonality of scandalous occasions and the increased eccentricity of climate models. This can lead to a decline in current and lower livelihoods in vulnerable regions. These progressions can also affect the cost of food globally. Creating countries and smallholder ranchers and pastoralists are, in particular, a rigid triumph over these modifications. A significant number of these small scale manufacturers are now adjusting to a corrupted ordinary asset base. They often need to learn about future decisions to adjust their frameworks for development and have limited resources and risk-taking capabilities to access and use innovations and money-related administrations.

Improving food safety while reducing environmental change and protecting the ordinary assets and environment administrations involves progress towards higher agricultural frameworks, making use of inputs much more lucrative, having less fluctuation and stronger returns, and more versatility towards risks, turmoil, and long haul atmosphere changeability. Increasingly profitable and stronger farming needs a remarkable step towards ensuring that land, water, soil supplements, and genetic resources are used even more efficiently. This step calls for significant modifications in the administration, the implementation, methods, and financial tools of domestic and neighborhood administrations. This shift also improves the access of manufacturers to company industries. These advances contribute substantially to the relief of atmospheric changes by reducing ozone depreciating substances discharges per unit of soil or possibly agricultural items and extending carbon sinks. Agriculture and food frameworks are subject to significant modifications to tackle the associated problems of food security and environmental change.

- Increasing asset skills are essential both for increasing and ensuring long-term sustainability safety and for reducing environmental change.
- Each type of hazard needs to be strengthened and modified to ensure its vulnerability.
- In each scale, and on ecological, economic and social grounds, efficiency and strength must be seen together.
- Brilliant agriculture can be a remarkable driver of a green economy and a strong method for implementing economic progress.
- Addressing the safety of food and environmental changes need all partners' deliberate and composite integration and long-term activities.
- Certifiably not yet another agriculture structure nor many methods are the shrewd climate agriculture. It is also an approach to handle the modifications needed in rural frameworks given the need to tackle food safety and environmental changes.

As defined and launched by the FAO at the 2010 Hague Conference on Agriculture, Food Security and Climate Change, smart agriculture (SA) connected with atmospheric circumstances contribute to the achievement of practical progress. The three components of maintainable progress (financial, social, and environmental) are coordinated by each other to face up to the difficulties of sustainability and climate. It consists of three main fields: a reasonable increase in profitability and wages for agriculture; adaptation and production of flexibility to environmental changes; ozone depletion or possibly evacuation outflows, if possible.

SA is the way to tackle the specific circumstances of strategy and speculation to achieve viable rural progress for food safety as a result of environmental changes. The size, rapidity, and magnitude of the consequences of environmental changes on agricultural frameworks make the far-reaching balance of these effects in domestic farming arrangements, undertakings, and initiatives essential. The SA strategy aims to acknowledge and implement maintainable agricultural improvements within the specific environmental variation parameters.

FAO and its accomplices are aware that making the modifications necessary for SA and summit these many destinations require an integrated methodology that is receptive to specific circumstances in the vicinity. The SA concept increases comprehensive global and national footing to tackle the problems of managing to farm under environmental changes, in cross-section coordination of agriculture fields, such as the cultivation of plants, domesticated animals, ranger service and fishing, for instance. SA is an idea that requires adjustment to contribute to food security and moderation in the techniques of rural development. Some countries around the world have announced their intention to obtain SA methods for addressing their agrarian divisions. However, there is a broad discrepancy over the SA concept, strategy, and its diversity use in the world. A gradually formal reason for SA's concept and philosophy is fundamental to assemble and in the meantime, to describe how the idea can be linked across a range of circumstances [2].

The enhancement of energy and water is essential to benefit from the potential cooperative energy sources, reduce exchange offs, and promote the use of ordinary resources and the administrations of the biological system. FAO's multiple offices worked together to verbalize the concept of the SA to tackle these complex tasks and strengthen the part of nationhood.

The methodology also aims to strengthen occupations and the safety of sustenance, particularly of smallholder farmers, by enhancing the management and use of periodic resources and adopting appropriate technological and progressive measures for the development, handling, and promotion of agricultural products. SA looks at the social, economic, and ecological environment where it is linked to increase the benefits and restrict trade-offs. Impacts on life and neighborhood assets are further assessed. The coordinated scenic tactics that follow the biological system norms of the board and viable soil and water use are an essential segment. SA seeks to assist countries to develop the key arrangements and aims to standard environmental changes in agriculture divisions by offering the assumption that practical agricultural development can be operationalized under changed circumstances. Combining and coordinating key strategy and institutional plans are also critical for use in creative finance instruments connecting and blending open and private atmosphere and agricultural resources. To expand practices in the atmosphere, the distribution of information, extensive support, and combination agreement take suitable organization and management aspects. It is not possible to achieve all SA destinations without a time delay. It must resolve explicit requirements and advantages and compromise [3].

It is a methodology that demands unequivocal evaluations to acknowledge suitable agricultural advances and procedures. SA is an exclusive and explicit agricultural innovation or practice that can be linked all around.

METHODOLOGY

1. Report on complicated interconnected problems of food safety, development, and environmental change and identify integrated decisions which benefit cooperative energy and lower offsets;

2. Perceives that the options are created by explicit national boundaries and social, economic and ecological circumstances in which they are linked;
3. Surveys the relationships between fields and the needs of the multiple partners involved;
4. Distinguishes selection limits, especially among farmers, and provides appropriate provisions for arrangements, methodologies, activities, and motivations;
5. Attempts to empower the parties by promoting strategies, budgetary speculations as well as institutional game plans;
6. Attempts to achieve distinct goals with the type that needs to be determined and group decisions ended with distinct benefits and exchanges;
7. Enhanced access to government, learning, inherited assets, financial goods, and markets, particularly for smallholders, should help to strengthen and improve vocations;
8. Addresses the adjustment and assembly of stunts, particularly those identified as environmental variability, as the effect of environmental variation has a significant agricultural and provincial improvement.
9. Contemplates environmental variation relief as a budding auxiliary co-advantage, particularly in low-salary, farming-based populaces;
10. They seek to identify opportunities for funding about the atmosphere and include them in traditional sources of the Farming Speculation Fund.

The agricultural and support framework must move forward and ensure food safety and as such, adapt to changes in the environment and distinctive weights of the asset and contribute to the relief of environmental variability.

Guaranteeing Nourishment Safety

There are still more than 870 million people estimated to be malnourished in 2010-2012 [5]. The world is generating adequate sustenance. Moreover, extra milliards of people lack fundamental micronutrients and are undernourished. The mystery is that meanwhile numerous people arc heavily consumed in most extravagant countries and that 60% of the undernourished are nutritious farmers, smallholder farmers, and pastoralists, while 20% live in metropolitan areas and 20% are people out of the nation. Food is not just a basic need for inferior manufacturers; it is the only and frequently sensitive reinforcement they have to maintain themselves. What is valid for families at the macroeconomic stage is also applicable. Thirty-two countries, twenty of them in Africa, face food shortages and need global assistance from crises. In many of them, horticulture is incomprehensibly a major, if not actual, part of the economy.

The goal is to guarantee nourishment and sustenance security around the world. Guaranteeing accessibility of calories and adequate worldwide generation isn't sufficient; we additionally need to ensure that enough sustenance is available to everybody, all over, physically and financially. Besides, we must ensure that the right quality and decent range are appropriately applied in this sustenance. The aim is to ensure the reliability of these three food supply and security sectors: accessibility, availability, and use.

By 2050, the population as a whole grow by 33%. The formed nations have a large share of the extra 2 billion. Meanwhile, more individuals live in metropolitan areas (70% compared to the present 50%). The use of animal products has been driven by increased urbanization and wages in developed countries [6]. With this trend in mind, FAO estimates that by 2050, manufacturing is rising by 60 percent to meet regular food and feed requirements [7]. Another vital factor in the world market is interest in bio-fuels based on national agreements and the development of the global interest. As the Organization of Economic Cooperation and Development (OECD) - FAO estimates indicate, biofuel generation in the range of 2005 and 2019 is twice as dependent as a result of growing orders and usage motivations [8].

Effects of Environmental Changes on Agribusiness

Agricultural businesses have been impacted by the environmental change now and are legally and implicitly depend on to continue to produce sustainability [9]. Mean temperature increase; downpour design modifications; extended variability, both in the design of the temperature and downpour; changes in the accessibility of water; recurrence and strength of exceptional occasions; sea-level rise and salt; biological system irritations, all having essential effects on agri-industry, ranger services, and fishing [10-11]. The extent of these consequences will not only depend on the strength and timing of the progressions but also depend on their combination, which is increasingly uncertain and under neighboring circumstances. Proper understanding of the impact of environmental change on agricultural business needs spatial data, tools, and models of real regions of generation. Since the 2007 Intergovernmental Panel on Climate Change (IPCC) report, many studies have sought to foresee and projected such impacts, enabling us to have a more strong view of expected changes [12-13].

PARKING

The leaving office has become a critical factor in the development of urban focuses throughout the globe since Ford Model-T owners have placed their cars in steed barns next to their cars. In most cases, private neighborhoods, car parking structures began as one story block structure. The first business type for manufacturing organized carports was housing in real cities, and most of the original carports were heated, enclosed structures with the common frameworks of windows. It was the lodges that disturbed and made carports a crucial part of the urban scene, mainly in cities such as

Chicago and New York. Chicago's Hotel LaSalle was one of the country's significant hotels to face the challenge at the end. A red block with staggered, unbearable carport with covered windows was manufactured to maintain out the gush and a slope to ensure quick halt. The inn called it "the finest carport in America."

Although cars were created in the nineteenth century, they did not come back to the heart until 1905, when many organizations manufactured "horseless wagons." Early cars moved into urban communities all over the location with cars, steeds, and trolls; the main route was inadequate to fit them all. Only one strategy was available: up. In the late 1920s, versatile vehicle paint finishes brought another real shift to the structure of the office. Vehicles could, without being harmed, be left outside in the downpour or snow medium-term, which led to carports with no windows. Despite the unbelievable discouragement that prevented the construction of new carports and subsequent World War II, new developments increased sharply in the late 1940s with the main carports. In new carports, the inter-floor tilt structure was the straight express path, with all cars left on floors. In the late 1940s, planned parking construction was reassessed and the parking entry ramps multiplied.

With the structure explosion of the 1950s, an external office park has long become the standard of stop-planning. Like administration stations, car park structure owners have shifted far away from the 100 percent valet model, intending to reduce operating expenses. The parking carport set up for–pay offices, as well as the personal parking structure, has been used at businesses. With the move away from offices, drastically lower job expenses, new parking structures were expanded for many administrations, which could not already handle the expenses of an organized stopping [14-15].

Parking – IoT

The probability of terrific urban schemes became known at an early stage. From now on, it is conceivable that the web improves the stuff that inspires the town. In the IoT sector, substantial efforts are being produced to assist urban foundations to be able and reliable. IoT tends to address issues such as traffic blockage, car restraint leaving working environments, and road achievement. Smart parking includes a zone connection of an IoT module used to monitor and signal the condition of accessibility for each stop area. A flexible application also allows an end customer to inspect the opening of the car park and make reasonable reservations for a stop opening. The Internet of Things (IoT) probability started with things with explicit contraptions in character. Contraptions can be searched, controlled, or monitored using Internet-related remote PCs. IoT develops Internet use, which provides correspondence between contraptions and tangible things or' things' in that capacity. The two remarkable IoT words are "web" and "things." Web proposes that servers, PCs, tablets, and mobiles, using displays and accomplice constructions used, should be gigantic in particular. The web enables information to be sent, received, or allowed. There are numerous professions and suggestions in English. The word "Thing" is used to refer to a physical article, an activity or thought, a situation, or an intervention if we do not want to be accurate. IoT contains everything from an action on contracts to physical matters; numerous papers may be available to collect data from distant locations and to be awarded to data management, control, management, and review units in policies and associations.

It creates a dream, in which things (wearable, ready-clock, home-goods, and things incorporated) become great, continue living through perception, readiness, and transmission through implanted small traps, which speak through frameworks with distant objects or individuals. The beautiful nature of cloud planning also enables engineers to be flexible. Make their apps and host them. Cloud is an optimal IoT partner, as it's like a point for verifying all sensor data from distant areas. These fragments led to two signs of progress being merged to improve another enhancement called the Cloud of Things(CoT). The things(nodes) in CoT could be accessed from any distant region via the nucleus, verified and monitored. Due to elevated cloud adjustment, any amount of focuses could be continuously combined or separated from the IoT framework. It is right to make a smart city that the ascent of the internet of things offers the chance to be conceivable. The main issue identified by sharp urban regions is the leaving of workplaces and heap-up traffic [16]. Today's city areas have been trying for riders to find a car park, and with the regularly growing amount of personal car customers, everything is becoming more difficult. This situation can be seen as an open passage for bright urban schemes to attempt to upgrade the feasibility of their ending assets together to reduce the number of occasions, stopping and road malfunctions. Issues regarding stops and stops can be resolved if drivers are told about openness in the parking places at their arranged destination and around the timetable. In trying to achieve low-control structures, there are non-stop advances in all kinds of impact models to provide the new Internet of Things apps.

Looked for by upgrades to improve sensors, distinct urban areas today have selected various IoT-based structures to be displayed within and around urban systems. An advanced evaluation by the International Parking Foundation reflects an increase in inventive in structural stopping. There are currently specific stop systems, which confirm that occupants pass constant information on open car parks. These buildings involve fit detectors to be sent in halt rooms to view the population as lively information management units to assemble first judgment parts from data aggregated over various sources. The excellent stop-frame is performed with effective cloud-connected implementation. The framework allows a customer to learn about parking transparency on an uninterrupted basis.

Prerequisite for IoT-Cloud Integration

IoT and Circled Enlisting have seen gigantic motion. Both developments have their core focus, regardless of the combination of two or three common trends. First of all, the mechanical goals of IoT can be met, for instance, by using the unbelievable limitations and resources of the cloud [15]. Then again, the cloud can extend its expansion in an equally vibrant and consistently dispersed manner, by using IoT, to administer certifiable substances. With its extraordinarily essential dimension, the cloud takes the bulk of complexities and functionalities needed to run the application more than halfway between stuff and apps. Next is a touch of the components that caused the cloud and IoT mergers.

Point of Confinement

The IoT includes multiple sources of data (things) that generate enormous amounts of information not manufactured or semi-handled. IoT, therefore, needs a large quantity of information to be collected, processed, viewed and shared [16]. The cloud makes it difficult, easy, and on-demand, so it is the best, most cost-effective, response with IoT-based data. The Cloud information index is available from anywhere via standard Application Programme Interface (API)s and can be imagined.

Check Control

The gadgets used under IoT require boundaries to be prepared. Data gathered from various sensors are usually transferred to much more important areas where their social opportunity and management are to be imagined [17]. The control requirements of the IoT can be addressed by the use of endless limits of preparation and cloud models on request. IoT structures can then conduct reliable data preparation with the help of adequate preparation and console extremely responsive apps.

Correspondence Assets

IoT's central handling is to talk to each other using a presented equipment strategy to Internet Protocol (IP) enhanced contraptions. Cloud supports trash and persuasive interface, track and coordinate gadgets from anywhere on the web [18]. IoT frameworks can reliably screen and regulate stuff through distant areas by using particular apps.

Adaptability

Cloud provides IoT with multifaceted technology. It provides a vibrant agreement for the development or reduction of assets. When cloud negotiation is given, any number of "things" can be fused or removed from the frameworks. The cloud adapts resources to the basics of stuff and apps.

Receptiveness

Whenever any location is accessible to favorable conditions, cloud negotiations are vital. With the cloud, apps are fully functional, and customers receive steady connections.

Interoperability

The use of different gadgets by IoT is consolidated. These gadgets can have distinct rigging or scheduling plans that cause similarity problems properly. It turns up to be exceptionally poorly arranged to ensure interoperability between these devices, in an IoT situation. Cloud leads this problem to look for, as it provides a typical type of relationship and relationship between distinct gadgets. Contracts may share a plan that is acceptable to them and trade data.

Shrewd Cities were fantasy to humanity continuously. Monstrous developments in the realization of sharp urban structures have been created over the years. Improving the Internet of Things and Cloud movements has brought new potential results in comparison to adequate urban schemes. The executive's framework has been at the point of convergence of vigilant urban domains with sharp stopping work settings and traffic [19-22].

LIGHTING

For the most portion of the chronological landscape of humanity, two light wellsprings were essentially open from the reasons for a man to the 18th century. The more settled the two are lights, the medium we see and the characteristics of which the eye has a balance over a long period and the second counterfeit light source, the flame, integrated during a substantial moment before the stone age, with its progress in social technologies and mechanical assemblies. From now on, lighting circumstances continued for a critical moment as before. The show-stopper in the Altamira sinkhole was also shown as Renaissance baroque craftsmanship under similar light [23-24].

Lighting has been forced into daylight and fire, and for this very reason, man has continued for numerous years to use these two light hotspots.

Natural Light

Due to the daylight, this reliably inferred altering structure forms the requirements for ordinary lighting. Thus, the recurrence of sun rays was acclimatized by entire buildings and individual rooms. Furthermore, the size of the rooms was dependent on natural lighting and ventilation. Phenomenal essential kinds of daylight structures recognized in the distinct climate zones of the world with lighting circumstances. We see the enhancement of buildings with huge, big windows in cold areas with the overwhelmingly cloudy sky, which enables as much light as could be normal because of the current scenario. It was discovered that diffuse glorious light made light uniform; problems inherent to glorious ordinary light, shadows, glare, and inside space overheating, could, moreover, be ignored for a couple of beautiful days a year.

These problems are crucial in nations with much ordinary light. In the smaller part of the structure, a more significant part of the constructions here have little windows; moreover, the exterior splitters are incredibly knowledgeable. This can only penetrate the structure by barely any fast ordinary light. The lighting today is affected by (1) the light that reflects from the surfaces of the structure, (2) the light is dissipated by the whole method of reflection and (3) its infrarouge portion is enormously dispersed. When asked whether there was enough light, up-to-date quality and cerebral perceptual study were considered in the same way as light supervision, which is evident in how compositional nuances are handled. Some parts were organized in particular to promote the spatial effect required through the trading of light and shadow by the available light.

The edges and flutter on pieces have a 3-dimensional impact indirect, prevalent light reliefs that pay little attention to whether they are of little importance. Such nuances involve higher importance for a comparative impact in diffuse light. In tropical countries, the facade, therefore, required simple, shallow surface structures, while the plan for something else in the north–and the internal structure–had to do with additionally explicit structures and emphasis by disguising the structure of the surfaces.

However, light is not just about the three-dimensionalization of spatial organs. It is an exceptional strategy to monitor our psychological measurement recognition. In ancient Egyptian paradise–for example in the sun asylum of Amun Re in Karnak or Abu Simbel–, light found not as uniform, including illumination, as techniques to emphasize what is fundamental–the well-ordered passages become darker in order for the watchman to change the image of the God according to low levels of light. [25-26].

Unnatural Light

An enhancement in the construction can function as an invaluable clock. Significant lighting effects occur on the first days or during specific periods during the year when the sun sets or otherwise sets or during the middle of the winter solstice. From the very beginning, a crest in the spots of a love of the Baroque era – for example, the Birnau adventure church or the Dominikus Zimmermann's trip church in Upper Bavaria, – has been devoted to deliberately isolating light effects. The visitor looks from the diffuse magnificence of the boat to the amazing.

A comparable approach of defencelessness also happens in the region of false lighting, which was linked to inadequate light sources. It came to a very apparent conclusion after a little time that it was a loose touch to select pieces of wood that particularly combustible and light produced, and particularly resinous pinewood displaced the branch.

In this phase, the marks element of the wood is not merely dependent on burning material to transmit even more light wrongly, notwithstanding the presence of devouring lamps. In these cases, selected revitalizers were used financially; the light holders were reduced to a wick as vehicle strategies for wax or oil. The increase of the oil and fire indicated that man at that time had insignificant, respectfully secure, lighting sources accessible to him.

The oil light produced in ancient occurrences dealt with the most critical type of light structure progress for a long time. Later on, the light itself was joined to by the fire. The flames and its wonderful strength, however, stayed unchanged in a variety of styles, with different kinds of high stone appliances and sconces.

This brilliant energy was inferior from existing light sources, and artificial lighting stayed a short apparatus. The brightness of the flamingo was always restricted to the instant situation rather than by daylight, which gave beautiful and isolated lighting for a whole room. People gathered around the section, which provided light or arranged it authentically next to the light. The light started to grave the night time of man, though weak. To beautifully lit up internal components after dull, it needed enormous quantities of costly lights and devices that were viable to wealthy visitors. Essential lighting, as we are probably aware, remained the prohibitive space of common light until the late 18th century [27].

Science behind Light

Either way or a different light is more confusing than energy. Whereas a first energy prologue allows us to use alone model or photograph, light requires different models based on the portion of the intrigue.

Isaac Newton suggested that "corpuscles" be light. The future communicated by radiant bodies in straight lines and would follow the retina of the eye. For particular optical structure angles straight line optics work admirably, especially where the sections are enormous, like mirror and center-point. The thinking was not legitimate, therefore. Huygens showed that light should have a wave of nature, supported by test outcomes of youthful and others. Impacts such as diffraction can not be further explained. It was found that the wavelengths were brief. There was a problem at that moment in showing from where did waves come, and how did the waves pass through a vacuum? Waves were seen as swells on water, or as weight waves in air. An all-invasive substance called the "ether" was suggested as the medium for transport.

The wave's hypothesis has a significant boost, and the ether disappears when James Clerk Maxwell suggested that it might be a sort of radiation. Electromagnetic radiation is considered a comprehensive range, and the noticeable light is a small part of it. Einstein, Planck, and others have shown, however, that a range of corpuscular hypotheses from the 20th century should be clarified by the electricity effect photography, where light flowing from certain materials could produce an electric flow. This current form was suggested as the quantum radiation hypothesis since it requires vitality only in defined parcels or quanta.

Actual material science unites both quantical and wave speculations by stating that however, Einstein, Planck, and others demonstrate that a range of corpuscular hypotheses must be clarified by the photograph electric effect, where the light falls on some of the substances can create electric flow. This new form was suggested as the quantum radiation hypothesis because it only requires vitality in characterized bundles or quantities. The light quantity was called a photon.

Everything has been proved by Einstein, Planck, and others, that a range of corpuscular hypotheses must be explained by the photograph of electric effect, whereby light on certain chemicals could cause an electric flow. This new form was offered as the quantum radiation hypothesis because it only needs to be vital in characterized plots or quantities. The light quantity has been called a photon. Today, material science also unites the quantum hypotheses of waves, expressing that every moving molecule of mass has a wave of its length concerning it.

Light Energy Management

The use of energy, as well as it's cost and effect on earth, is a general problem. As human instinct is what it is, here is another scenario where lip administration is paid in a "correct" natural way. Lighting control can contribute significantly to saving vitality, but it is necessary to express a warning. Where the illumination scheme has complicated lighting management for stylish purposes or even for earthly purposes, it should be conceivable to plan its job to make the most efficient use of energy.

The Electromagnetic Spectrum

The electromagnetic spectrum contains different types of transverse waves. All of these waves can undergo interference, be reflected, refracted, diffracted and polarised, and travel at the speed of light, 2.998 x 10⁸ m/s, in a vacuum.

Longer Wavelength → Shorter Wavelength

Lower Frequency → Higher Frequency

Type	Radio Waves	Microwaves	Infrared (IR)	Optical (visible) Light	Ultraviolet (UV)	X-rays	Gamma Rays
Wavelength (m)	$>1 \times 10^{-1}$	$1 \times 10^{-1} - 1 \times 10^{-3}$	$1 \times 10^{-3} - 7 \times 10^{-7}$	$7 \times 10^{-7} - 4 \times 10^{-7}$	$4 \times 10^{-7} - 1 \times 10^{-8}$	$1 \times 10^{-8} - 1 \times 10^{-13}$	$<10^{-11}$
Frequency (Hz)	$<3 \times 10^{9}$	$3 \times 10^{9} - 3 \times 10^{11}$	$3 \times 10^{11} - 4 \times 10^{14}$	$4 \times 10^{14} - 8 \times 10^{14}$	$8 \times 10^{14} - 3 \times 10^{17}$	$3 \times 10^{17} - 3 \times 10^{19}$	$>3 \times 10^{17}$
Energy (J)	$<2 \times 10^{24}$	$2 \times 10^{24} - 2 \times 10^{22}$	$2 \times 10^{22} - 3 \times 10^{19}$	$3 \times 10^{19} - 5 \times 10^{19}$	$5 \times 10^{19} - 2 \times 10^{17}$	$2 \times 10^{17} - 2 \times 10^{14}$	$>2 \times 10^{14}$
How Are They Made?	By oscillating electrons in aerials	Directly produced by electron tube oscillators	By oscillating molecules in hot objects, such as LEDs, flames and stars	Emitted by the sun and other very hot objects, such as light bulbs and laser pointers	Emitted by the sun and other extremely hot objects, such as sparks and UV lamps	By firing electrons at a metal target	Emitted during radioactive decay
Applications	Television, radio, communications	Radar, cooking, satellite communications, mobile phones	Night vision, heat used in toasters and grills, remote controls, thermal imaging	Seeing, communications, optical fibres, DVD players, laser printers	Sunbeds, invisible security marking, sterilisation	X-ray photography, CT scanning, airport security, cancer treatment	Irradiation of food, security, cancer treatment, sterilisation
Dangers	Not thought to be hazardous	Heats water within the body, can damage or kill cells	Felt as heat, can cause skin damage and burns	Can damage the eyes	Can cause sunburn, damages eyes, causes cancer	Damages eyes and cells, causes cancer	Damages eyes and cells, causes cancer
How Are They Detected?	Resonance in electronic circuits using an aerial	Resonance in electronic circuits, heating effect on water	Thermometer, thermopile, heating effect on skin	Photographic film, the eye, photodetectors	Photographic film, sunburn, photodetectors	Photographic film, fluorescence	Photographic film, Geiger-Müller tube

Figure 1. Electromagnetic Spectrum. Courtesy: Education Charts by Daydream Education [29].

In any case, it is crucial to verify the compensation figures when it comes solely for the sake of a low vitality to introduce an outstanding lighting control (rather than a straight-forward, physically exchanged institution). There was a bad venture compensation for some unpredictable PC regulated frameworks. [30-33].

RESULTS AND CONCLUSION

The chapter concludes with essential elements of daily life intending to meet Industry 4.0 expectations. The most critical elements of human existence are Smart farming, Lighting, and Parking, which aim to make life durable and comfortable. Frameworks of agricultural generation confront increasing competition for limited common resources from distinct fields. The accessibility and quality of these resources are also affected by unsustainable management rehearsals and changing climate and climate circumstances. In response to these circumstances, the agri-business divisions must enhance their manageability and adjust in ways that do not negotiate globally to ensure food safety for everybody to the impacts of environmental changes. These problems are personally and inseparably linked and should always be addressed. The world's rapid urbanization has brought energy to the concept of "brilliant urban regions."

The shift of urban regions to lively urban communities provides an exceptionally open door to improve the welfare of indigenous people and to encourage economic progress. The vision of a bright town was an idea for all metropolitan regions continuously. Over the years, efforts have been made, and thinking has been used to achieve this in many countries. The Internet of Things is an essential innovation alongside cloud computing. Smart Parking is a key administration to be a beautiful town. Previous technologies have been misused, which have been either inefficient or too expensive. The major sections are the sensors used to identify the car. The deliberate use of light to achieve an effect down to earth or pleasing affect is the lighting. Daylighting is now and again used as the fundamental source of light in constructions through daytime (using windows, lovely windows, or light retreats). This can save one's energy rather than using false lighting, which speaks to a significant portion of the use in constructions of energy. Legitimate lighting can enhance tasks, enhance the existence of land, or have beneficial mental implications for the people.

REFERENCES

[1]   *Food security and agricultural mitigation in developing countries: options for capturing synergies.* FAO. 2009, Rome.

[2]   Climate Change, Agriculture, and Food Security (CCAFS) & Consultative Group for International Agricultural Research (CGIAR). 2013. *CCAFS & CGIAR website.* (available at http://www.ccafs.cgia r.org/).

[3]   *Modelling System for Agricultural Impacts of Climate Change* (MOSIACC). (available at http://www.fao.org/climatechange/mosai c).

[4]   Hedger, M., Mitchell, T., Leavy, J., Greeley, M., Downie, A. & Horrocks, L. 2008. *Desk review: evaluation of adaptation to climate change from a development perspective. Institute of Development Studies.*

[5]   FAO. 2012. FAO policy on cash-based transfers. Rome.

[6]   FAO. 2009a. *The state of food and agriculture: livestock in the balance.* Rome.

[7]   Conforti, P., eds. 2011. *Looking ahead in world food and agriculture: perspectives to 2050.* Rome, FAO.

[8]   OECD & FAO. 2010. *Agricultural outlook 2010-2019.*

[9]   Lobell, D., Schlenker, W. & Costa-Roberts, J. 2011. *Climate trends and global crop production since 1980.* Science.

[10]   Gornall, J., Betts, R., Burke, E., Clark, R., Camp, J., Willett, K. & Wiltshire, A. 2010. Implications of Climate change for agricultural productivity in the early twenty-first century. *Philosophical Transactions of the Royal Society B-Biological Sciences,* 365: 2973– 2989.

[11] Beddington, J., Asaduzzaman, M., Clark, M., Fernández, A., Guillou, M., Jahn, M., Erda, L., Mamo, T., Van Bo, N., Nobre, C. A., Scholes, R., Sharmam R. & Wakhungu, J. 2012b. *Achieving food security in the face of climate change: final report from the Commission on Sustainable Agriculture and Climate Change.* Copenhagen, Denmark, CGIAR Research Program on Climate Change, Agriculture, and Food Security (CCAFS). (available at www.ccafs.cgiar.org/commission).

[12] Intergovernmental Panel on Climate Change (IPCC). *2007a. Climate change 2007: impacts, adaptation, and vulnerability,* M. L. Parry, O. F. Canziani, J. P. Palutikof, P. J. van der Linder & C. E. Hanson, eds. pp. 869-883. Cambridge University Press.

[13] IPCC. 2007b. Climate Change 2007: mitigation, B. Metz, O. R. Davidson, P. R. Bosch, R. Dave & L. A. Meyer, eds. Contribution of Working Group III to the Fourth Assessment Report of the IPCC. Cambridge, United Kingdom, and New York, USA, *Cambridge University Press.*

[14] *Guide to Design and Automated Parking Facilities, Automated & Mechanical Parking Association (NPA),* Washington, D.C., AMPA and NPA, February 2003.

[15] Botta, A., de Donato, W., Persico, V., & Pescapé, A. (2014, August). On the Integration of Cloud Computing and Internet of Things. In *Future Internet of Things and Cloud (FiCloud),* 2014 International Conference on (pp. 23-30). *IEEE.*

[16] Rao, B. B. P., Saluia, P., Sharma, N., Mittal, A., & Sharma, S. V. (2012, December). Cloud computing for Internet of Things & sensing based applications. In *Sensing Technology (ICST),* 2012 Sixth International Conference on (pp. 374-380). IEEE.

[17] Zaslavsky, A., Perera, C., & Georgakopoulos, D. (2013). *Sensing as a service and big data.* 1301.0159.

[18] Suciu, G., et.al., Smart cities built on resilient cloud computing and secure internet of things. *In Control Systems and Computer Science (CSCS),* 2013 19th International Conference on (pp. 513-518). IEEE.

[19] *Fast Park System* website, http://www.fastprk.com.

[20] Zheng, Y., Rajasegarar, S., & Leckie, C. (2015, April). Parking availability prediction for sensor-enabled car parks in smart cities. In Intelligent Sensors, Sensor Networks and Information Processing (ISSNIP), *2015 IEEE Tenth International Conference* on (pp. 1-6). IEEE.

[21] Rico, J., Sancho, J., Cendon, B., & Camus, M. (2013, March). Parking easier by using context information of a smart city: Enabling fast search and management of parking resources. In *Advanced Information Networking and Applications Workshops (WAINA),* 2013 27th International Conference on (pp. 1380-1385). IEEE.

[22] Ji, Z., Ganchev, I., O'droma, M., & Zhang, X. (2014, August). A cloud-based intelligent car parking services for smart cities. In *General Assembly and Scientific Symposium* (URSI GASS), 2014 XXXIth URSI (pp. 1-4). IEEE.

[23] Bentham, F., *The Art of Stage Lighting.* Pitman, London 1969.

[24] *Birren, Faber, Light, Color and Environment.* Van Nostrand Reinhold, New York 1969.

[25] De Boer, J. B.; Fischer, D.: Interior Lighting. *Philips Technical Library*, Antwerp 1981.

[26] Erhard, Louis: Views on the Visual Environment. *A Potpourri of Essays on Lighting Design* IES 1985.

[27] Kaufman, John E. ed., *Illuminating Engineering Society Lighting Handbook Reference Volume.* IES,1981.

[28] Lam, William M. C.; Beitz, Albert; Hallenbeck, G. H.: *An Approach to the Design of the Luminous Environment.* MIT, Boston, 1976.

[29] *Education Charts* by Daydream Education.

[30] *Lighting Technology Terminology.* BS 4727, 1972.

[31] D. C. Pritchard. *Addison Wesley Longman, Lighting.,* 5th Edition 1995.

[32] Mark S. Rea, *Lighting Handbook, Illuminating Engineering Society, of North America,* (IESNA), 9th Edition 2000.

[33] Carl Gardner and Barry Hannaford. Lighting Design. Subtitled "An Introductory Guide for Professionals" *The Design Council* (UK) 1993.

In: LoRA and IoT Networks …
Editors: A. Gehlot, R. Singh et al.

ISBN: 978-1-53617-164-8
© 2020 Nova Science Publishers, Inc.

Chapter 5

WIRELESS PERSONAL AREA NETWORK-BASED WASTE MONITORING SYSTEM USING XBEE AND IOT

Shaik Vaseem Akram, Rajesh Singh[1], and Anita Gehlot[2]*

SEEE, Lovely Professional University, Jalandhar, Punjab, India

ABSTRACT

Smart sensors and low power wireless communication have made it easier to build a smart system. By using smart sensors and low power wireless communication, we can enhance existing waste management practices. In this, we are proposing an architecture based on the XBee module and the Internet of Things for monitoring the garbage bins. Here the XBee based sensors which are deploying in the garbage bin initiates the functioning of our architecture. The sensor data of the garbage bin communicates to the local server with the assistance of the XBee module.

---

* Corresponding Author's Email: vaseemakram5491@gmail.com.
[1] Corresponding Author's Email: srajsssece@gmail.com.
[2] Corresponding Author's Email: eranita5@gmail.com.

The local server integrates with NodeMCU and communicates the sensor data to the central server through the internet. After receiving the information from the local server, the central server will analyze the data and responds. Hence the proposed architecture will enhance traditional waste management practices.

Keywords: XBee, NodeMCU, and Internet of Things (IoT)

INTRODUCTION

Waste management is an important authority in an urban context for collecting, cleaning, and maintaining the cities clean and green. When we look after traditional waste management practices, they are consuming much time and money too. Due to the practice of the traditional methods, the cities are still facing the problem of the overflow and bad smell. For enhancing the waste management practices, there is a necessity of mechanism which can enable the bins to communicate automatically to nearby authorities. Previous studies proposed a different kind of mechanism for improving waste management. In the initial stage, RFID (Radio Frequency Identification) based system is being proposed for monitoring the waste. However, RFID is not reliable for a long duration because harsh environmental conditions will cause damage quickly. With the advent of wireless sensors, some studied proposed wireless sensor network-based mechanism for waste management. The proposed system is not enough for enhancing waste management.

The previous communication protocol is capable of communicating in one direction only. However, to build and provide intelligence to the bin, this kind of communication protocol is not sufficient. By taking advantage of wireless sensors and the internet, the internet of things concept came into existence, where the devices can be monitored wirelessly from any place. In the internet of things, the information is communicating to the cloud server through Wi-Fi or GPRS. This cloud server will analyze the data and send it to the user to make a decision. However, in some cases, the municipal authorities are far away from the garbage bins, and it becomes difficult to collect the waste on time. To overcome all these challenges, we are proposing an architecture which consists of two types of server for monitoring the waste. In this study, the XBee based sensor is installing in the garbage bins, and it communicates the sensor information from the bin to the nearby local server. This local server is assisting with Node MCU for communicating the information to the central server through the internet. The central server will collect the data, analyze the status of the bin, and respond.

PRIOR ART

Hong *et al.* (2014), a smart garbage system aims to reduce food waste. This smart garbage system works on the wireless mesh network for communicating the bins with each other. For monitoring the garbage bin, the information of sensors transmits to a local server [1]. Anagnostopoulos *et al.* (2015), addresses the proposal of the internet of things for dynamic waste management. For solving the problems of real-time monitoring of waste management, a top-k query-based scheduling model using sensors and data streams is proposed [2]. Gutierrez *et al.* (2015) & Hasan et al. (2017), The Internet of Things (IoT)-based prototype proposes for waste monitoring and this prototype consists of sensors that can read the garbage level data in a bin and transmit it to nearby local authorities via the internet [3, 8]. Wen *et al.* (2018), The Internet of Things (IoT) based system aims to solve the problem of food waste management in the town of Suzhou (China). The RFID (Radio Frequency Identification) reader and weight Measurement Sensors are mounting in trash bins for real-time monitoring [4]. Abdullah *et al.* (2018), introduces a unique design for collecting waste in an urban area. Separate trucks are designed to collect different types of waste using the Internet of Things (IoT) [5]. Omar *et al.* (2018), a solid waste management system (SWMS) proposed for enhancing waste management practices, and this system work on RFID, GPS (Global Positioning Satellite), and GPRS (Global Packet for Radio Service) [6]. Lella *et al.* (2017), for achieving the optimal result in the collection and transportation of waste, a method based on GIS (Geographic Information System) and network analysis is proposed [7]. Aazam *et al.* (2016), Sensors and a communication protocol are installing in the bins for communicating the level of the waste in the bin to the cloud server. These bins are connecting to the cloud server for real-time monitoring [9]. Rohit *et al.* (2018), an ultrasonic sensor is embedding in the bin for detecting the level of waste. With the help of Esri's ArcGIS software communication, transport efficiency in waste management is enhanced [10]. Chaudhary *et al.* (2019), improving waste collection and transportation efficiency by applying Esri's ArcGIS 3.2 software [11]. Castro Lundin *et al.* (2017), proposed a system for enhancing waste management, and it works on wireless sensor networks and cloud. LoraWAN based wireless protocol assists the cloud server [12].

PROPOSED ARCHITECTURE

Waste management plays a vital role in smart cities for creating a sustainable environment. The main theme of a sustainable environment is to build such an environment that does not affect the existing natural resources. When it comes to waste management, there is a need for a system that can reduce transport costs, time-saving, and environmental pollution. For meeting these requirements, we are proposing a system based on XBee wireless communication for monitoring the garbage bins through the internet of things. Figure 1. Represents the main architecture of the proposed system for monitoring the garbage bins and figures represents for 'n' number of bins. The components that are present in the main architecture are:

1) XBee based smart sensor
2) Local server
3) Main server

XBee is a wireless personal network based on IEEE 802.15.4 standard (WPAN) for point-to-point wireless communication, and the XBee radio module works on the principle of Zigbee technology. It can communicate to more than 100m without any interruption. In the present context, the smart system should able to consume low power and provide maximum output for communication. Here XBee wireless communication consumes low power for communication. Different kinds of sensors are integrating with XBee for transmitting the status of the bin to the local server. The sensors can be an ultrasonic sensor for level measurement, an infrared sensor for object detection, and a temperature sensor for measuring the temperature of the garbage bin. An ultrasonic sensor is useful for sending the level status of the bin, the infrared sensor helps in opening the lid according to the object detection, and the temperature sensor assists in analyzing the temperature level of the bins.

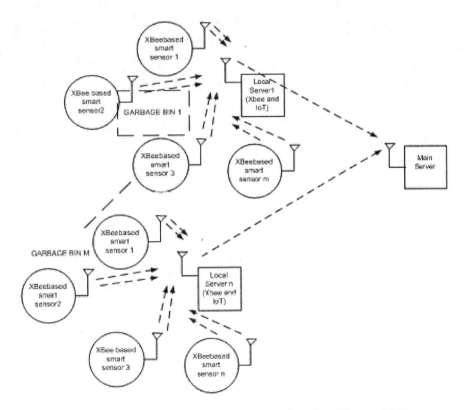

Figure 1. Architecture for monitoring of garbage bins based on Xbee and IoT.

XBee Based Smart Sensor

XBee based smart sensor is the main component of the architecture because the functioning of the main architecture initiates from this sensor. Here the sensor of the garbage bin will communicate to the local server about the status of the bin

Figure 2. Represents the block diagram of the XBee based smart sensor and the main components that exist in the XBee based smart sensor are:

1) Sensors
2) Display
3) Microcontroller
4) Power source
5) XBee modem

The sensor is the device that measures the change in the physical properties of the environment and communicates it to near devices. LCD (Liquid Crystal Display) is used to display the information of the bin, the information displayed will be the level and ID of the bin.

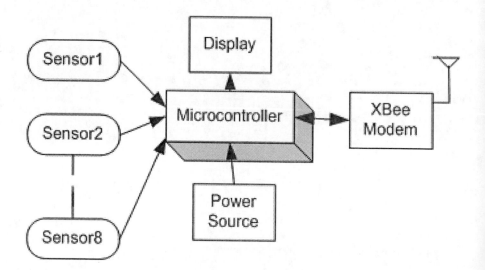

Figure 2. XBee based smart sensor.

XBee modem inserts in the smart sensor for enabling point-to-point communication.

XBee modem helps in communicating serial, and also it helps in communicating with the intelligent devices wirelessly. Fundamentally, embedded devices powers with a battery source. So to meet the requirements of embedded devices, there is a necessity of low powered wireless communication. Here XBee module will be able to fulfill the requirement of the embedded devices.

Local Server

In some contexts, the main municipal authority will be far away from the city. Due to a lack of municipal authority near to the garbage bins, the garbage bins overflow. Due to the overflowing of garbage bins, the surroundings get polluted and smells bad. This problem can be solved by installing the local server near the bins. Here local server receives the sensor information from the garbage end and transmits it to the central server.

Figure 3 presents the architecture of a local server with NodeMCU. The components that exist in the architecture of the local server are:

1) XBee Modem
2) NodeMCU
3) Microcontroller
4) Power source
5) Display

For communicating to the central server, the local server requires a new network to transmit the information from its end to the central server. To make it possible, NodeMCU is assisting in this architecture.

NodeMCU is an open Internet of Things (IoT) platform that is integrating with the ESP8266 Wi-Fi modem for enabling communication over the internet.

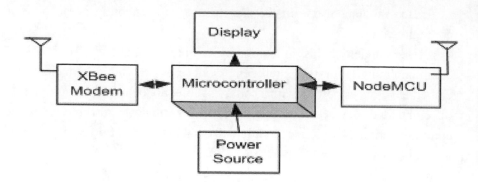

Figure 3. Architecture of Local SERVER with NodeMCU (ESP8266).

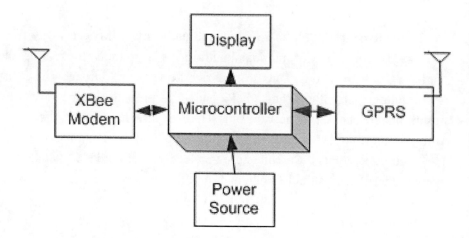

Figure 4. Architecture of Local server with GPRS.

Figure 4. Represents the architecture of the local server based on the GPRS (Global Packet for Radio Service) radio module. Due to the absence of Wi-Fi connectivity, GPRS comes into action for transmitting the information wirelessly.

As GPRS is available in a wide area, it can help in transmitting the information to a long distance. The local server assists the GPRS in transmitting the information.

After receiving the information from the sensor through XBee, it is the responsibility of the local server to enable communication to the central server for analyzing and act.

Main Server

Figure 5 Represents the architecture of the central server. The central server is useful for receiving information from the local server. Received information from the local server will consist of the status of a bin; the status of the bin represents the level of the garbage in the bin. After receiving the information, the central server will analyze the information act according to the necessity. As the information stored in the central server, it will be easy for municipal authorities to plan a better strategy for collecting waste and enhance the existing waste management. Even it helps in planning for better management of transport, and it saves time and transport costs too.

The primary functioning of the architecture initiates from the XBee based smart sensor. The smart sensors sense the garbage bin, and if anything exceeds the threshold level, then the smart sensor starts communicating the sensor information to the nearby local server through the XBee module. XBee module communicates multiple devices at a time and transmits the information over a range of 100 meters with a radio frequency of 2.4 G.Hz. Now the local server received the information from the XBee based sensor about the status of the bin. The local server consists of the XBee modem for receiving the information from the transmitting garbage end. Due to the presence of NodeMCU, the information from the local server communicates to the central server through the internet. Here the internet access is possible because of ESP 8266 Wi-Fi modem in the local server.

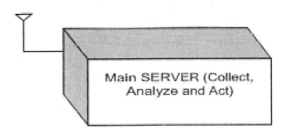

Figure 5. Architecture of central Server.

However, in some contexts, due to the absence of the Wi-Fi connection, GPRS will communicate the information of the bin from the local server to the central server. Now it is the responsibility of the central server to receive the information from the local server. Concerning the information received from the local server, the central server will analyze the information and act. As the central server is with the municipal authority, it is the responsibility of authorities to take immediate action to collect the waste. As the information is available with authorities, it is easy for the government and authorities to formulate policies to enhance the present waste management.

CONCLUSION

Waste management plays a vital role in building a clean and green environment. However, due to traditional practices, the municipal authorities are unable to maintain the cities neat and pollution-free. Here we need an advanced mechanism for enhancing waste management. With the availability of intelligent wireless sensors and advanced wireless communication protocol, we can build an advanced mechanism for achieving the targets of a sustainable environment. In this study, we proposed an Internet of Things (IoT) and XBee module based architecture for monitoring the garbage bins. Due to the presence of the internet of things, from any place, we can monitor the garbage bins. As the data is available in the central server, it is easy for authorities and the government to constitute new policies for enhancing waste management.

REFERENCES

[1]   Hong, Insung, Sunghoi Park, Beomseok Lee, Jaekeun Lee, Daebeom Jeong and Sehyun Park. "IoT-based smart garbage system for efficient food waste management". *The Scientific World Journal*, 2014 (2014).

[2]   Anagnostopoulos, Theodoros, Arkady Zaslavsy, Alexey Medvedev and Sergei Khoruzhnicov. "Top--k Query Based Dynamic Scheduling for IoT-enabled Smart City Waste Collection". In *2015 16th IEEE*

International Conference on Mobile Data Management, vol. 2, pp. 50 - 55. IEEE, 2015.

[3] Gutierrez, Jose M., Michael Jensen, Morten Henius and Tahir Riaz. "Smart waste collection system based on location intelligence". *Procedia Computer Science*, 61 (2015): 120 - 127.

[4] Wen, Zongguo, Shuhan Hu, Djavan De Clercq, M. Bruce Beck, Hua Zhang, Huanan Zhang, Fan Fei and Jianguo Liu. "Design, implementation, and evaluation of an Internet of Things (IoT) network system for restaurant food waste management". *Waste management*, 73 (2018): 26 - 38.

[5] Abdullah, Nibras, Ola A. Alwesabi and Rosni Abdullah. "IoT-Based Smart Waste Management System in a Smart City". In *International Conference of Reliable Information and Communication Technology*, pp. 364 - 371. Springer, Cham, 2018.

[6] Omar, M. F., Termizi, A. A. A., Zainal, D., Wahap, N. A., Ismail, N. M., and Ahmad, N. "Implementation of spatial smart waste management system in malaysia". In *IOP Conference Series: Earth and Environmental Science*, vol. 37, no. 1, p. 012059. IOP Publishing, 2016.

[7] Lella, Jaydeep, Mandla, Venkata Ravibabu and Zhu, Xuan. "Solid waste collection/transport optimization and vegetation land cover estimation using Geographic Information System (GIS): A case study of a proposed smart-city". *Sustainable cities and society*, 35 (2017): 336 - 349.

[8] Hasan, B. M., Yeazdani, A. M. M., Istiaque, Labib Md., and Chowdhury, Rafee Mizan Khan. "*Smart waste management system using IoT*". PhD diss., BRAC University, 2017.

[9] Aazam, Mohammad, St-Hilaire, Marc, Lung, Chung-Horng and Lambadaris, Ioannis. "Cloud-based smart waste management for smart cities". In *2016 IEEE 21st International Workshop on Computer Aided Modelling and Design of Communication Links and Networks (CAMAD)*, pp. 188 - 193. IEEE, 2016.

[10] Rohit, G. Sai, M. Chandra, Bharat, Saha, Shaurabh and Das, Debanjan. "Smart Dual Dustbin Model for Waste Management in Smart Cities".

In *2018 3rd International Conference for Convergence in Technology (I2CT)*, pp. 1 - 5. IEEE, 2018.

[11] Chaudhary, Shailendra, Nidhi, Chaitanya and Rawal, Nek Ram. "GIS-Based Model for Optimal Collection and Transportation System for Solid Waste in Allahabad City". In *Emerging Technologies in Data Mining and Information Security*, pp. 45 - 65. Springer, Singapore, 2019.

[12] Lundin, Castro, André, Ali Gurcan Ozkil and Schuldt-Jensen, Jakob. "Smart cities: A case study in waste monitoring and management". In *Proceedings of the 50th Hawaii international conference on system sciences*, 2017.

Chapter 6

ROLE OF FIRE SAFETY ENGINEERING METHODS AND DEVICES IN PRESENT SCENARIO: A REVIEW

Rajesh Singh[1,], Anita Gehlot[1,†], Rohit Samkaria[2,‡], Shivam Kumar[3,§] and Bhupendra Singh[4]*

[1]Lovely Professional University, Punjab, India
[2]IIT, Kanpur, India
[3]University of Petroleum and Energy Studies, Uttarakhand, India
[4]Schematics Microelectronics, Dehradun, India

ABSTRACT

Fire is one of the major causes of disaster not only in the developing countries but also in developed countries. Fire is an essential element for humans, but when it is uncontrolled it causes havoc to the mankind. Fire leads to losses in terms of lives, property and environment. Past accident

---

[*] Corresponding Author's Email: srajssssece@gmail.com.
[†] Corresponding Author's Email: eranita5@gmail.com.
[‡] Corresponding Author's Email : rohit.samkaria93@gmail.com.
[§] Corresponding Author's Email : shivam.kasauli@gmail.com.

analysis reveals the fact that the majority of industrial accidents happen because of human error. A number of the natural events, like forest fires, start and escalate into the major disaster due to lack of timely human intervention. In this context, the ability to have complete automation of critical safety features of any processes, would appear to be a boon. Over the past decade, a number of embedded technology assisted systems have been proposed to monitor fire situations. This paper presents a comprehensive review on fire safety model, framework and systems. It is concluded that the sensor and microcontroller based fire safety systems can be used to monitor the fire prone areas and generate an alert alarm. Moreover, the paper also identifies various areas where fire safety technology upgradation is required. The importance of wireless sensor network as one of the efficient methods for fire safety system is also highlighted.

Keywords: fire safety, sensor, wireless sensor network, embedded systems

INTRODUCTION

Almost 1-1.25% of global GDP loses has been estimated globally due to fire. In the fire cases, the majority of deaths are due to smoke inhalation. Almost 65-70% of deaths occurred due to smoke inhalation, while rest are due to severe fire burn. Fire investigation analysis results shows that the majority of fire incidents are due to the exposure time. Exposure time not only delayes the evacuation of people but it also increases the intensity of fire as well as surface areas which cost in terms of lives and property. In-depth forensic analysis of the past accidents reveal the fact that the majority of industrial accidents happen because of human error. Natural incidents like forest fire often escalate out of control because of late detection, resulting in delayed response. Often lack of information about the nature of fire and the response of structure, under onslaught of fire, results in death of personnel involved in firefighting as happened at Piper Alpha in 1999, World Trade Centre (WTC) collapse in 2002, and King cross fires in 1992 (Berry, Dave, et al., 2005). Instead of blaming the helpers and engineers, requirement of precise and better technology needs to be explored.

Fire is the process of oxidation of the material in combustion which results in the release of heat, light and other reactive products. To start the combustion fuel must be heated up, to the ignition temperature. To start the process of combustion, three components are required, which include heat, fuel and oxygen. This combination is known as the fire triangle. The fuel reacts with the oxygen to produce the heat and light. The burning process is caused due to the movement of loose heated molecules. The fire sustains with the heat generated by the reaction and fire keeps burning if enough oxygen and fuel is available [https://www.sciencelearn.org.nz]. The combustion is mainly categorized in two forms, one is complete combustion and other incomplete combustion. In the complete combustion only water and carbon dioxide is released by burning of the fuel with blue flame and no additional products like smoke is produced. The example of complete burning is methane gas for cooking at homes. Incomplete combustion is caused due to unavailability of proper oxygen during the reaction which results in yellow or orange colour flame and release additional products like carbon, carbon monoxide, carbon dioxide, smoke and water [http://www.i cdo.org].

Disaster is an event occurred accidently or due to natural catastrophe which results in the unfortunate consequences, including loss of life, economic lose and environmental loss. Disaster is categorized into two types, one is natural disaster and other is man-made disaster. Man-made disaster is caused due to the negligence in human actions and natural disasters is natural process of earth results in the adverse events like- floods, hurricanes, tsunamis, earthquake, Avalanches and landslides, sinkholes, Blizzards [http://www.disastermgmt.org]. Fire disaster is among the type of disasters which can be man-made and natural both. Fire disaster includes incidents of fire in tunnels, aircrafts, buildings and forest. Fire disaster in homes are due to negligence of human which is caused due to smoking, candles, electrical appliances, short circuit, barbeques etc.

Depending on the type of fuel, fire is classified in five classes. The classification makes it easier to choose the type of extinguisher [http://www.eurofireprotection.com].

Table 1. Classification of fire

Class	Type of fire	Material Involved	Type of Extinguisher
Class A	Ordinary combustible fires- It is due to supply of heat to continue the burning process.	Paper, wood, rubber, textile, plastic and organic carbon	Water based or form fire extinguisher to cut the heat supply.
Class B	Flammable liquids- ignition temperature less than 100^0C	petrol, kerosene, alcohol, solvents and paints	Foam fire extinguisher to smother the flames. Avoid water as it will spread the fire.
Class C	Flammable gases- little spark is enough to ignite.	butane, propane and petroleum gases	It is most dangerous type of fire for which most fire extinguishers are ineffective, the only method is to isolate gas supply or use dry powder extinguishers.
Class D	Metal fires-lot of heat is required to ignite	Alkali metals such as potassium, magnesium, aluminium and sodium can burn when in contact with air and water.	Specialist type D powder fire extinguishers suitable for use on metal fires but avoid water as it will increase the fire.
-	Electrical Fires-	Short circuits, overloaded switchboards, faulty equipment and damaged wiring	Isolate the supply of electricity. Carbon dioxide and dry powder fire extinguishers are the only types of fire extinguishers recommended for it. Don't use water or foam as they will increase the electric conductivity.
Class F	Cooking oil fires	cooking oil and fats	Wet chemical extinguishers, especially for class F, don't use water on it

Table 2. Types of Fire Extinguishers

Type of fire Extinguishers	Effective on	Avoid on
Water based	Class A	Class B, Class C, Class D, Class F
Foam based	Class A, Class B	Class C, Class D, Class F
CO2 based	Class A, Class B, Class C	Class D (results vary with type of metal)
CFC based	Class A, Class B, Class C, Class D	Class D (results vary with type of metal)
Dry Chemical based	Class A, Class B, Class C	Class D (results vary with type of metal)

Table 3. Firefighting strategy

Fire Situations	Firefighting strategy
Smothering a fire	In case Cloths of somebody catches fire then wrap the person in blanket and roll on ground
Letting it die	Isolate the fire from combustible material and oxygen, it will die.
Fire in pantry area	In case fire on oil/ghee then switch off the stove and simply cover the container to discontinue oxygen supply to it
Class C	If correct extinguisher is not available then convert it into Class A by turning off gas supply but don't use water
LPG Cylinder fire	Put water on base to cylinder. Keep the cylinder standing upright, stay away from it.
Smoke around	Crawl on the floor and try to exist the place

Although the type of extinguishers can be identified depending on the classification of the fire, yet depending on the circumstances the firefighting strategies may vary. Table shows the firefighting strategy according to the conditions.

FIRE SAFETY MODELS AND FRAMEWORK

ZHAO, Ling, et al. (2009) proposed a system to detect the nuisance created due to false alarm and missing reports. The system comprises of humidity and temperature sensors, which are placed in the forest to detect fire effectively [25]. De Rademaeker, Eddy, et al. (2014) concluded experts and scientist gathering to seek the technical improvement and scientific support for safe industry and quality life [43]. Yoon, Ik Keun, et al. (2011) demonstrated a framework which can enhance the job safety. Detailed hazard configuration for job safety analysis is also included [36]. Martin, Helmut, et al. (2017) discussed the role of interconnection in automated driving system and challenges of fault which may cause the failure [38]. Cheung, Sai On et al. (2004) proposed a safety and health monitoring system in construction called CSHM. This CSHM model helps to take management decisions with respect to hazards which may cause injurious accidents [5]. Figure 1 shows the conceptual frame work of the CSHM.

Mohamed, Sherif. (2002) proposed a research model on the basis of hypothesis for safe work behaviour. This model was tested with structural equation modelling. The results were concluded on the basis of tests [11]. Figure 2 shows the research model for the safety climate.

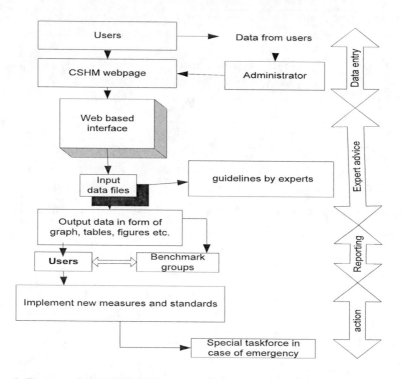

Figure 1. Framework for CSHM [5].

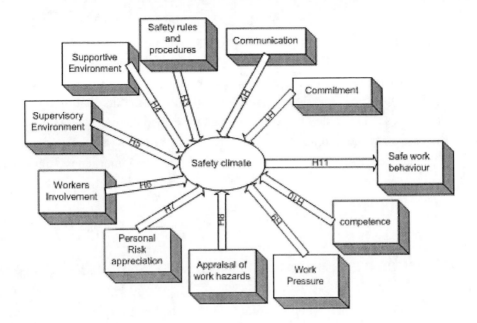

Figure 2. Safety Climate Model [11].

Kaiser, Bernhard et al. (2007) concluded the results for hazards and the failure with the role of safety models for software and hardware behaviour. A hybrid model named state/event fault tree was proposed. Quantitative evaluation of model was achieved with the help of simulation for case study on fire alarm system [13]. Yang, K. T. (1999) concluded that the fire codes application was increased for the fire safety designs in the buildings [14]. Birgit Östmana et al. (2017) discussed the material choice for building construction and concluded the timber not suitable from the fire safety point of view due to its high combustibility [61]. Søren Madsen et al. (2016) proposed a structural fire safety model resulting in optimized topology for load carrying capability [62]. Carlee Lehna et al. (2016) proposed a study to evaluate the effects of education programs on fire safety on homes in US. The purpose of the study was to educate the older adults about the safety [63]. Margrethe Kobes et al. (2010) discussed about the importance of safe escape from building in case of fire. Paper also included the human behaviour in fire [64]. Croce, Paul, et al. described the technical issue of international significance for fire safety research community by

International Forum of Fire Research Directors where the FORUM regulations, design, code for fire safety application discussed [67]. Novak, Jeremy, et al. Examine the role of the workspace relationships in employee's safety where they create RE (Resilience Engineering) and monitor behave of the employees in various organizational culture factors that affect these employees [71]. Ackley, H. Sprague et al. described the method that utilizes the data entry method used in various workspace to generate the emergency signal. They utilize two methods to generate the emergency signal i) Barcode Scanner to generate the signal ii) Emergency speech input, both the signal are network connected [72].

INTEGRATED EMERGENCY RESPONSE AND FIRE SAFETY

Berry, Dave, et al. (2005) discussed about the fire consequences and lack of information about the conditions which can cause deaths of hundreds of fire fighters like Piper Alpha explosion in 1999, world trade centre collapse in 2002 and king cross fires in 1992. Paper discussed the challenges and solutions for them [1]. Mishra, Manish Kumar et al. (2017) explained that the cost and energy savings are prominent issue in today scenario and BEMS (Building energy management systems) can help to control the various active systems such as lighting including artificial lighting. It can be further extended to the integration of different building systems [49]. Upadhyay, Rochan, et al. (2008) discussed the performance of wired and wireless monitoring systems for more efficient operations. A Zigbee based system was proposed to improve the safety quality. The need of more efficient system was also discussed with the applications of sensors [56]. Figure 3 shows the safety model and Figure 4 shows the Fire Grid system architecture.

An integrated fire emergency response system named "FireGrid". Zeng, Yuanyuan, et al. (2009) proposed a low cost solution based on wireless sensor network for the building automation. A study on communication protocols was done to find the suitable technique to improve fire evacuation [29]. Brailsford, Sally C., et al. (2004) proposed a review for on demand health care and emergency in Nottingham (England). The results were concluded on the basis on the interviews of 30 people and a conceptual. Study showed 1% less occupancy of bed per annum, on small number of admission from the general practice [60].

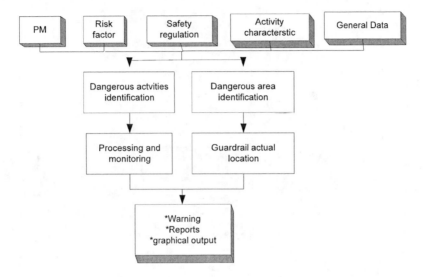

Figure 3. Safety model [56].

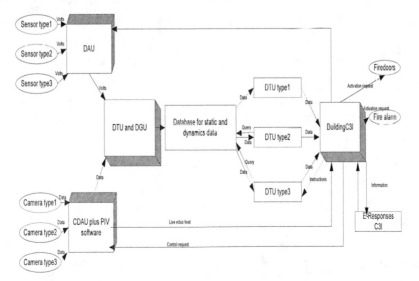

Figure 4. FireGrid system architecture [56].

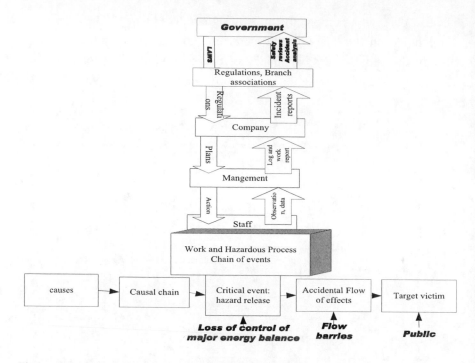

Figure 5. Socio-technical model of system operations [2].

Tseng, Wei-Wen, et al. described the survey of the released from the ministry of Health and Welfare that there are multiple small hospitals which can provide a 99 bed to the patients and have not properly deals with the safety managements and emergency evacuations for immovable patients. So idea is to merge these various hospitals with the large existing hospitals [75].

Nelson, Kellen N., et al. simulated the fire behavior in 24 year old lodgepole pine stands in Yellostone National Park, Wyyoming, US. They utilize operational parameterized with empirical fuel characterstics [106]. Bongiovanni, Ivano, et al. conduct study for managerial practices for the large paediatric hospitals to mitigate the consequences of major fire emergency and to restore the normal business. They categorized the major factors such as complexity of the undeleyed stakeholder network, several temporal and spatial constraints [76]. Santos-Reyes, Jaime et al. present the various result of the analysis of the emergency response for the 1996

Channel Tunnel Fire accident. The relevant associated with the deficiencies have been highlighted in the model [77].

ACCIDENTAL MODEL FOR SAFETY SYSTEMS ANALYSIS

Leveson, Nancy (2004) discussed a new approach towards accident and hazards analysis to understand the accidents causes and its preventions. Instead of blaming the helpers and engineers, requirement of precise and better technology was discussed [2].

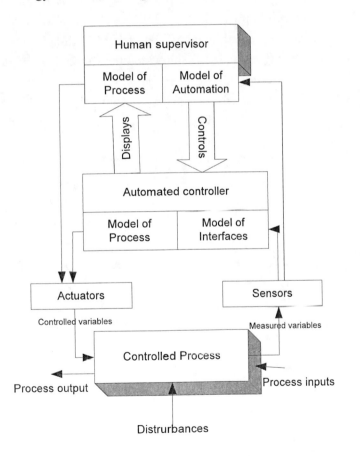

Figure 6. The control & process model [2].

Panesar-Walawege et al. (2011) proposed an integrated approach including UML profiles and model driven engineering. The concept is helpful to establish a relation between safety standards and application domain [27]. Acharyulu, PV Srinivas et al. (2015) discussed a study on new proposed framework for safety assessment. The study included the risk factors and significance of risk and result shows better improvement as compared to existing assessment techniques [28]. Sadvandi, Sara et al. (2012) discussed about the study of engineering tools for safety- security systems. Both are categorized and relation between two was explained. The role of system engineering on this issue was also discussed [31]. Ho, Chao-Ching et al. (2011) proposed a multi-sensor fusion based fire detection and fighting system, to improve the functionality. Paper also discussed the use of machine vision sensor reduces the delay of fire detection [41]. De Rademaeker, Eddy, et al. (2014) suggested the role of European Federation of Chemical Engineering (EFCE) in delivering sustainable processes and products [43]. Piriou, Pierre-Yves et al. presents the enriched fault tree for the dysfunctional behaviour of its components by using the Markove processes in an integrated manner for critical structures and Moore machine have been planned to ensure the safety [78]. Magnognou, Brady, et al. focus on the assessment of an ignition riskthat marely occurred due to the large unburned fuel gases. The study includes the initial well ventilated fire, subsequent decay during under ventilated and exhaust of unburnt gases [79]. Van Weyenberge, Bart, et al. describe the development of a risk assessment methodology that quantify the life safety risk and the important aspect of QRA (Quantitative Risk Analysis) the variability of various design parameters [80].

SAFETY AND SECURITY CRITICAL SERVICES IN BUILDING AUTOMATION AND CONTROL

Zhang, Sijie, et al. (2011) explored the problem faced by the safety engineers due to lack of information about hazardous conditions. This gap in the information flow is due to the separate planning team for construction industry and safety. Still the safety planning depends on the past experience and manual observations which can cause error in the calculations. A safety tool was proposed which may help in reducing the no. of accidents [6].

Novak, Thomas et al. (2010) proposed a new model for Building automation and control system, which combines the security and safety both. Paper discussed the basics of BACS with maintenance and management issues of the efficiency of the system [3]. Novak, Thomas et al. (2007) explained that the modern automated buildings are having two important components control system and building automation. As these systems deals with the safety, security and health of people, they need to be reliable and secure [18]. Kriaa, Siwar, et al. (2015) addressed a design and risk assessment, for security threats in digitalization of all the control systems [20].

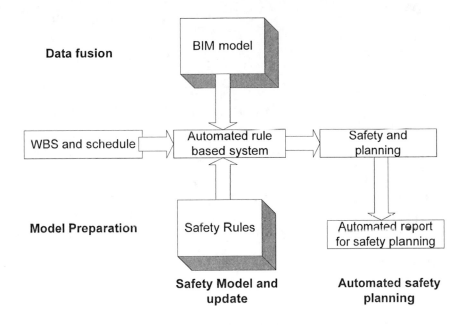

Figure 7. Framework for Safety System [6].

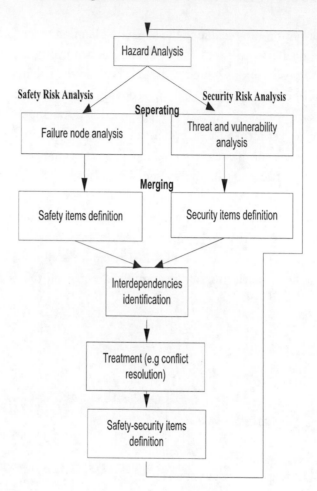

Figure 8. Safety security integrated risk analysis process [20].

Lehto, Mark R et al. (2009) described the guidelines and recommendations to control the hazards, so that warning can be generated for people placed at risk locations [34]. Obirailo, Oxana (2014) discussed the role of SAS in the petroleum processes. It is important because failure in the SAS can cause serious hazards [39]. Stewart, Robert John et al. configured a firing mechanism and fire sensor on the Wireless Sensor Network over a short range RF with a network hub that include a subscriber Identity for the module to be configured and to communicate with the server [65]. Cheng, Min-Yuan, et al. combine BIM to develop BIM-based intelligent fire prevention and disaster relief system that consist of five different modules and these system utilize the early warning, detection and real time evacuation [66].

FIRE DETECTION SYSTEMS AND ALGORITHMS

Xueli, Chen et al. (2010) designed a wireless sensor network based remote control for fire control [33]. Agarwal, Aditya, et al. (2017) proposed a system which included exact location identifier, fire detector and RF system. Author suggested that the study is very significant for countries like India where 50% of forest is fire prone [50]. Ramya, V et al. (2012) designed a system which was capable of monitoring the toxic gases and alcohol in the vehicle and sends an alarm signal to authorized person through GSM, in case of any critical situation [22]. XU, Zhi, et al. (2008) proposed a new and better anti jamming ability algorithm, for the embedded systems with high accuracy. Paper discussed the complications in the implementation of the algorithm on embedded system with restricted resources [4]. Kumaran, S et al. (2012) discussed the role of controlled area network in the fire extinguish for triggering the actuator [37]. Singh, Rajesh et al. (2010) suggested a wireless sensor network based real time temperature monitoring system for bus bar junction. Paper showed the possibility of long distance temperature monitoring of bus bar junction in real time [45].

Singh, Rajesh et al. (2011) suggested the role of wireless sensor networks (WSNs) in various applications. The sensor node sensed and stored the data and the mobile network can be used to transfer data. It has possible application in area of environmental monitoring [46]. Meera, C. S., et al. (2015) suggested the use of wireless sensor network technology to protect huge areas such as college campus or industrial area. A centralised wireless fire control system was developed for five dangerous areas and a direct communication channel sends immediate signal in case of fire in any area [47]. Teja, GNL Ravi, et al. (2014) shared the study of land slide detection system by integrating Geo-physical sensors. It has been developed at bidholi, Dehradun [48]. Gould, J. S., et al. measure the different methods to measure the time and speed of that travel and the experimental method depend upon the scale, location required accuracy and resources available [105].

Gwynne, S., et al. (2001) explained that the presence of smoke may not only evacuation strategy. The different type of adaptive behaviours were introduced with new capabilities. The behavioural data was collected from the real fire incidents in UK and USA. EXODUS is proposed as suite of software tools for evacuation simulation for large number of people [59].

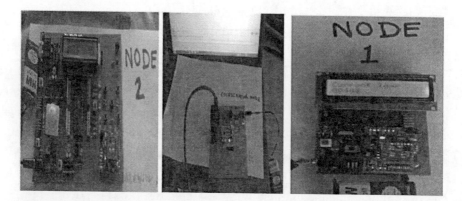

Figure 9. Homogeneous System [45].

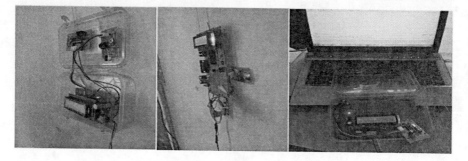

Figure 10. Sensor node, Control room node and data acquisition [48].

Vijayalakshmi, S. R. discuss the IoT framework for the fire monitoring, firefighting, planning. This research provides the development points of IoT in firefighting, Monitoring field [68]. Alam, Md Fasiul, et al. described the AV/VR (Augment and Virtual Reality based Internet of Things prototype for performing maintenance task in quit challenging and complex enviormentdue to underground facilities, uneasy access and various human and machine factors [69]. Shinde, Reshma, et al. describes the various techniques which have been already used in the fire safety like image processing and sensors used for fire detecting using CCTV footage [70]. Garcia-Jimenez, Santiago, et al. proves the literature of various fuzzy inference mechanism that are based on fuzzy variables and various fuzzy rules to obtain solutions. Mamdani inference algorithm proposed by using overlap function [82].

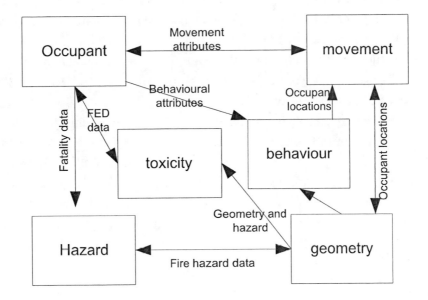

Figure 11. EXODUS modules [59].

FOREST FIRE SURVEILLANCE

CHEN, Xiao-juan (2007) proposed an image processing based fire detection system. The process included the collection of real time fire images and on the basis of changes fire can be detected [12]. ZHAO, Ling, et al. (2005) designed a wireless sensor network based fire monitoring system. The system comprised of humidity and temperature sensors, which were placed in the forest to detect fire effectively [25]. Xueli, Chen et al. (2010) proposed a smart fire monitoring and controlling fire system for the fire prone sectors of the forest. A wireless sensor network based system was designed to achieve remote control [33]. Agarwal, Aditya, et al. (2017) described a system which can sense the forest fire in its initial stage and provided data to control room from each tree. This system included exact location identifier, fire detector and RF system [50]. Costafreda-Aumedes, et al. analysis the various human factors causing fire in forest and developed fire occurrence modelling that aim to identify more appropriate variables and application in the fire management and civil protection [104]. González-Jorge, H., et al. describe the potential of UAS (Unmanned Areial System for preventing forest fire especially those are caused by the human intervention. Tey focused on the operational possibilities of the USA "AtlantikSolar" developed by ETH Zurich [81].

Wu, Jiping, and Yuenian Li. Described the early warning system foe the forest using infrared thermal imaging technology that consists of camera erected in the forest. The camera module includes frontal temperature detection and alarm signal [83]. Amanatiadis, Angelos, et al. developed the system for high altitude detection task and patrol the borders and woodlands where a lot numbers of ambiguous activites are not captured by the Unmanned Aerial Veichles. So they developed the "Hellenic Civil Unmanned Air Vehicle" [84]. Ye, Shiping, et al. describes the Roboust Satellite Technique for fire detection and monitoring. They also emphasis on the multi-temporal change detection technique and its application to data of SEVIRI to Meteosat Second Generation Platform [86]. Hua, Lizhong, and Guofan Shao present the overview of the various principles and case studies of various forest fire monitoring system with satellite and drone-mounted infrared remote sensing and this study includes the various FFM relevant IRRS algorithms, fixed threshold method, spectral method and multi temporal method [87].

Table 4. Comparison table for safety Systems

Ref.	Author	Year	Technique Used	Basis Used	Domain	Controller/Model Used/Software/ Technology	Hardware	Communication
[2]	Nancy Leveson	2004	STAMP (Systems-Theoretic Accident Model and Processes) Model	Accident Models	General Safety	STAMP	Automatic Controller, Actuators, Sensors	NA
[3]	Thomas Novak	2010	BACS (Building automation and Control Systems)	Network security & System security	Buildings & HVAC	NA	Gateway	NA
[5]	Sai on Cheung	2004	My SQL Database & PHP programming Languages	Health & Safety Parameters	Construction Safety	PHP, MySQL & Layer open SSI	Computer/ Laptop	NA
[6]	Sijie Zang	2011	3D Visualization & 4D Simulation	BIM (Building Information Modelling)	Construction Safety	BIM, VDC (Virtual Design & Construction Technology), SMC (SolibriModel Checker)	ABSE-NT	NA
[9]	Carl Hartung	2006	Wireless sensor-FireWxNet	Environmental Conditions & Topographical features	Wildland fire	CSMA, TCP/IP, WAP, MANTIS operating system	Satellite Transceiver, Radios, Solar Panels, Camera, sensor networks & LED	GOES, WIMS

Table 4. (Continued)

Ref.	Author	Year	Technique Used	Basis Used	Domain	Controller/Model Used/Software/ Technology	Hardware	Communication
[10]	Dimitris Kiritsis	2003	Smart Embedded Systems & Information Models [PEID (Product embedded information devices) & RFID IC]	Life cycle assessment	Product lifecycle management	PEID, RFID, CAD/CAM, DMS, PHM	PEID &RFID	GSM/ZIGBEE/ XBEE/CDMA/B LUETOOTH/RF ID/WIRELESS
[11]	Sherif Mohamed	2002	Structural Equation Modelling (SEM) & SEM technique Partial least squares (PLS)	Questionnaire	Construction Safety	SEM (Structural Equation Modelling)	NA	NA
[13]	Bernhard Kaiser	2007	SEFTs (Safe/Event Fault Trees)	FTA (Fault Tree Analysis)	Safety Analysis Model	Fault tree, DSPN's, SAFECOMP, ROOM (Realtime object oriented modelling), MC (Markov Chain-Probabilistic state-based model), CFT's (Component Fault Trees), TimeNET	NA	NA
[14]	K. T. Yang	1999	Simulation using Zone & field Models	Fire Codes	Fire Safety	FLUENT, SOFIE, FLOW3D, UNDSAFE & KAMELEON	NA	NA

Ref.	Author	Year	Technique Used	Basis Used	Domain	Controller/Model Used/Software/Technology	Hardware	Communication
[15]	Dietmar Dietrich	2010	Fieldbus Systems	BA (Building Automation), SM (Smart Home)	Buildings	WSN, AI (Artificial Intelligence)	NA	NA
[17]	V. Ramya	2012	Wireless networks	Embedded system	Hazardous Gas Detecting & Alerting	PIC Microcontroller, RTMS (Real Time Operating System), Embedded C	LCD Display, Gas sensor, LPG sensor, Combustible gas sensor, ADC (Analog to digital Convertor)	GSM
[18]	Thomas Novak	2007	BACS (Building automation and Control Systems)	BACS	Safety & Security Assurance in building	BACS	NA	NA
[19]	Ramy Nazier	2012	Fault tree	Risk driven behaviour model	Software intensive systems safety	State Based Behaviour Model, State Charts	NA	NA
[20]	Siwar Kriaa	2015	Risk Assessment process	ICS (Industrial control systems)	Industrial Safety	Graphical modeling, GSN, NFR, BDMP, BBN, CHASSIS, MBSE, STAMP	NA	NA

Table 4. (Continued)

Ref.	Author	Year	Technique Used	Basis Used	Domain	Controller/Model Used/Software/ Technology	Hardware	Communication
[21]	M. A. Hannan	2008	Embedded Vehicle safety system	ISS (Intelligent Safety Systems)	Vehicle Safety	CAAS (Collision and accident avoidance system), PCI, DAQ, PCM (Precise Collision Model), Borlabd C++	PCI (Peripheral Component Interconnect), DAQ (Data Acquisition)	DAQ Card, Display unit, Sensor
[23]	Qinqin Chen	2014	Bow-tie-analysis	Environmental risk management	Petrochemical Industry	Environmental risk assessment model, PIERSMS (Petrochemical industry environmental risk source management system)	NA	NA
[24]	K. Padma Priya	2014	WSN (Wireless sensor networks)	Embedded system	LPG leakage monitoring system for home safety	Keil software, PIC microcontroller, ATMEGA168 microcontroller & Zigbee	ARM 7 Processor, Alarm, MQ-5 gas sensor, LED indicator, buzzer, LCD	GSM

Ref.	Author	Year	Technique Used	Basis Used	Domain	Controller/Model Used/Software/Technology	Hardware	Communication
[26]	Mohammad reza Akhondi, Alex	2010	WSNs (Wireless sensor networks)	WSN applications	Oil, Gas and Petrochemical Industry	RFD (Reduced Function Device), FFD (Full Function Device)	RFD, FFD, IC, Sensors, SCADA	TDMA (Time-division multiple access), SOM (Self Organising Map), CDMA, GPRS, DTU (Data Transfer Unit), LAN, RTU (Remote Terminal Unit)
[27]	Rajwinder Kaur Panesar	2011	PES (Programmable Electronic System)	MDE (Model Driven Engineering)	Safety	UML Class Models	NA	NA
[28]	P. V. Srinivas Acharyulu	2015	System automation	Safety-critical systems	Power Plant	SCADA	PLC	NA
[30]	K. Sahulhameed	2013	Human operating fire system	Autonomous Robot	Fire Extinguishing	Embedded Systems, Image Processing, MATLAB, Keiluvision	Robot, Multiple sensors, Alarms, Web Camera with Laptop, Moving Platform, Pump with PWN Unit	NA

Table 4. (Continued)

Ref.	Author	Year	Technique Used	Basis Used	Domain	Controller/Model Used/Software/ Technology	Hardware	Communication
[35]	Sudipta Bhattacharjee	2012	WSNs (Wireless sensor networks)	Wireless Sensor Network & Simulation	Fire Safety in coal mines	ARENA Simulation Software, Trans receiver Module, Sensing module	NA	NA
[43]	Eddy De Rademaeker	2014	Loss Prevention	Risk Management	Process Safety	CAD	NA	NA
[44]	Ferhat Babur	2016	-	OH&S (Occupational Health & Safety)	Ship Building Industry	Fine Kinney Model, Matrix Model (5*5)	NA	NA
[45]	Rajesh Singh	2010	WSNs (Wireless sensor networks)	Wireless Sensor Network	Temperature Monitoring	RF Transceiver, Microcontroller, Sensor Network	Power Supply Unit, Sensing Module, Micro Controller, LCD Module, Zigbee Transceiver module, PC, ADC (Analog to Digital Converter)	Peer to Peer
[46]	Rajesh Singh	2011	WSNs (Wireless sensor networks)	Wireless Sensor Network	Pressure Monitoring	AVR Microcontroller	Zigbee Transceiver module, pressure sensor, Power Supply Unit, Micro Controller, LCD Module, PC	Slave Node

Ref.	Author	Year	Technique Used	Basis Used	Domain	Controller/Model Used/Software/Technology	Hardware	Communication
[47]	Meera C. S.	2015	WSN (Wireless sensor networks)	Fire Alarm Safety	Fire Safety	SHT 11 Modules	LCD Screen, ATMEGA32 Controller, PC	Nodal
[48]	G. N. L. Ravi Teja	2014	WSN (Wireless sensor networks)	Heterogeneous Network	Landslide Detection	Zigbee module, DAS (Data Acquisition system)	Geophone, presure sensor, moisture sensor, strain gauge, tilt sensor, ATMEGA-16, MAX232, USART (Universal synchronous Asynchronous receiver transmitter)	Ethernet, Wifi, satellite
[54]	M. Victoria Moreno	2014	IOT (Internet of things)	BMS (Buiding management system)	Smart Building	SCADA, HAM (Home automation module)	Zigbee, EIBUS/X10 devices, serial com devices, CAN Nodes, sesors	NA
[55]	Wen Tsai Sung	2011	Wireless sensor-FireWxNet	Power Supply Unit, Sensing Module, Micro Controller, LCD Module, Zigbee Transceiver module, PC, ADC (Analog to Digital Converter)	Industrial measurement and monitoring	Lab View	Zigbee Transmitter, LVDT (Linear Variable Differential Transformer)	Wireless Transmission

WEATHER CONDITION MONITORING IN THE FIRE ENVIRONMENT

Hartung, Carl, et al. (2006) designed a system with sensor network, to analyse the performance and observations. The system is based on FireWxNet and designed to monitor the weather conditions [9].

Figure 12. Enclosure for sensor nodes [9].

Figure 13. Smart system for gas cylinder [24].

Sharma, Sajal, et al. (2016) suggested a multi-rotor unmanned aerial vehicle which includes a system for real time video transfer, temperature sensor and smoke detecting unit. It can help in real time monitoring of environment. Its use can be extended in object delivery, surveillance and research [51]. Qinqin, Chen, et al. (2014) explained the resources of environmental risk are identified and classified on the basis of consequences and management costs. A web GIS based management system is designed and developed [23]. Ramya, V. et al. (2012) designed a microcontroller based safety system to detect the toxic gases. If level of hazardous gas extent beyond the threshold level then a message is sent to authorized person for quick response, in case critical situation [17]. Priya, K. Padma, et al. (2014) designed a system to detect the LPG leakage. In case of emergency power supply is shut down and a SMS is sent [24]. Feo-Arenis, Sergio, et al. (2014) discussed the design flaws in the fire alarm system and suggested an improved design. Study showed the verification of the fire systems was possible for enterprises, to improve the product quality [32]. Bhattacharjee, Sudipta, et al. (2012) designed an early warning system for emergency cases. The system was capable of sensing the fire and generates the alarm to save the lives [35]. Pereira, Mário Gonzalez, et al. examines the the different role of the fir in the socio-ecological history of the Mediterranean type ecosystem and gave emphasis on the interaction between the fire and climate [88]. Chu, Thuan, Xulin Guo et al. evaluated the multiple factors in Larch forest in Siberia that influencing patterns of variability in a post fire and analze a time-series of remote sensing to estimate post fire recovery [89]. Hamadeh, Nizar, et al. uses various correlation methods like stastical regression, Spearman, Pearson and Kendall's Tau correlation to identify the most affecting parameters on the fire ignition during the the last six months in the forest of the North Lebanon. These correlations are studies in order to develop the fire danger index [90].

VEHICLE SAFETY

Hannan, M. A., et al. (2008) proposed a sensing algorithm based intelligent safety system, for automobiles. The frontal collision data is collected with pneumatic device. On the basis of collected data a sensing algorithm is proposed and developed for automotive applications [21].

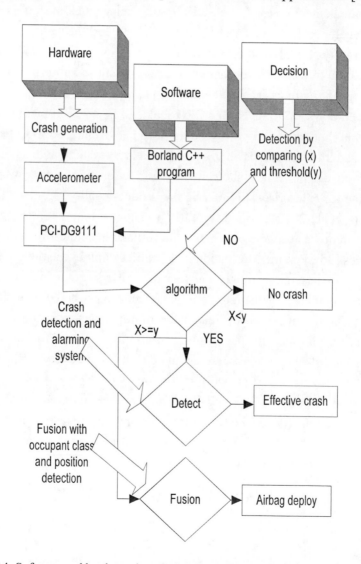

Figure 14. Software and hardware interfacing flow diagram [21].

Ramya, V., et al. (2012) proposed an embedded system based safety module for the vehicles. The system is capable of monitoring the toxic gases and alcohol in the vehicle and sends an alarm signal to authorized person through GSM, in case of any critical situation [22]. Martin, Helmut, et al. (2017) discussed the role of interconnection in automated driving system and challenges of fault which can cause the failure [38]. Reza Akhondi, Mohammad, et al. (2010) discussed the role of wireless sensor network in the industries like refineries, petrochemicals, oil and gas, which is used to monitor the health and safety related issues [26]. Johnson, Randy S. develop a Vehicle safety belt that incorporates video camera, processor, face detection software, safety belt whre processor detects the human face and IR emits the output that is positioned with the seat belt so when processor didn't receive indication of occupied seat that trigger the safety belt bypass warning indicator [99]. Axelsson, Jakob has studied the Vehicle platooning with aim to improve traffic thought the existing infrastructure. Author stsuty the known fact about the safety of the platooning including analysis methods [100]. Zhao, Ding, et al. proposes an accelerated approach for evaluation of Automated Vehicles before their release and deployment as the currently existing techniques N-FOT is very time consuming and the result result are used to generate the motions of the other primary vehicles to accerlerate the verfications of AV in simulation and various controlled experiments [101]. Koopman, Philip, and Michael Wagner gives the various safety approaches that need to be ensure in the autonomous vehicle across all the levels of the functional hierarchy. These includes from hardware fault tolerance to resilient machine learning [102].

PRODUCTION LIFE CYCLE MANAGEMENT, HEALTH AND SAFETY ETC.

Kiritsis, Dimitris et al. (2003) discussed an embedded information device with complete flow management. It is required to close the information loop for the product from the producer to the customer [10].

Babur, Ferhat et al. (2016) suggested that OHS-(Occupational Health and Safety) insures safety of employee, production and business. It can help in reducing the occupational disease and accidents in workplace [44].

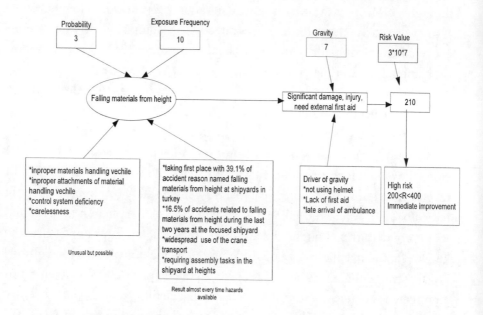

Figure 15. A risk schema event [44].

Shukla, Abhinav et al. (2017) described a LabVIEW based data logger which can collect data for parameters such as terminal voltage, current, power factor, input power etc. Proteus simulation is developed of check accuracy [52]. Gupta, Tanisha, et al. (2017) proposed a system to indicate the level of radiation leakage for nuclear power plant. It starts alarm which would be indicated the high level of radiations. LabVIEW GUI is also designed as data logger [53]. Nazier, Ramy et al. (2012) discussed an approach to integrate the fault trees into state based behaviour model. The results of the model enables the automated generation of some test cases [19]. Walser, Tobias et al. assessed the risk of various chemical substances to the human health and to our environment. They also categorised the role of the Conventional risk assessment (RA) that are limited to their scope. They utilise the three methods that allows the robuist search for sustainable alternatives that have an unfavourable risk profile [97] Lybbert, Andrew H., et al. study the sexual reproductive success in plant-pollinator systems and found that the flower production of the wind and generalist pollilnates plansts were greater effect and production increase then the unburned area and whereas the some specialist species response were natural [103]. Bonfiglio, Annalisa, et al. (2011) discussed the need of safety and its awareness among the public, specially for the fire fighters and rescuers [8]. Dietrich, Dietmar, et al. (2010) described an introduction to building automation with smart homes. The other areas of automation are also discussed. Paper also shows the role of sensor and actuator in the automation along with the scientific challenges [15]. Sun, Qi-bo, et al. (2010) discussed the basic concept of IoT with its features. It also compared the IoT with the features of ubiquitous network and machine to machine systems. Finally an IoT based proposals are suggested [16]. Moreno, M. Victoria et al. (2014) designed an IoT based intelligent system to improve individual ability to rule the actuators of the system at their service. The energy saving reflected in initial stage is about 23% [54]. Sahulhameed, K., et al. (2013) described the development of an autonomous robot, which is capable of detecting fire using image processing and also can rescue [30]. Apvrille et al. analyze the role of communicating and autonomous devices in the future Public Safety Networks which merely focus that the information should reach in fast way to recues and rescucrs should not have to concern themselves about the their autonomous mission so as not to delay but assist them efficiently [73]. Shakdher, Arjun et al. have created VANETs (Vehicular Ad-hoc Networks) to provide the information to doctor of the patients arriving to the hospitals via ambulance vehicle so that precious life can be saved as many developed countries people dies due to the delay medical response [74]. Cerqueira, Diogo et al. study the accuracy of the smartphone based on the illuminance measurement and the sample taken from nine mobile phones from three different platform Android, iOS and Windows and almost 14 aaps were selected for testing [94]Bianchini, Augusto, et al. have introduced the Efficacy Index foe effective implementation of the an OHSMS (Occupational Health and Saftey Management System. The study determined the effective implementation of the system and aim was to define a procedure to demonstrate the exemption of responsibility of company in case of any accident [95]. Tchiehe, Derrick Nanda et al. indexed the risk influential factors fin domain of OHS and suggest the topology for the samewhere they incorporate total 8 parameters regrouping 19 criteria and 14 variable that basically influence the risk acceptability [96]. Smith, Meredith Y., et al. asses the benefit risk profile in the medicinal product where to increase the transparency in the decision making process the paper seeks approach i0 how to integrate lifecycle to embed such process ii) key issue to anticipate iii) best practice and lesion learned [98]. Di Giuseppe, Francesca, et al. conclude the negative effect of the Salvage Logging (SL) on soil plant system. They analysed soil sample immediately after the treatment i.e., microclimate conditions and some soil properties [91]. Šturm, Tomaž, and Tomaž Podobnikar evaluated the Severity mapping methods for a low intensity, patchy prescribed fire in south-eastern Austalian eucalypt forest [92]. Bayne, Karen et al. has proposed the WSNs to managed the forest in future by collecting the real time data and at the same time helping to better understand complex relationship of forests [93].

CONCLUSION

Fire safety system is a necessary part of any organization including educational institutes, hospitals, industries, forest, buildings etc. History is witness for the loss of lives due to fire accidents occurred at public places. Research reveals that, majority of fire deaths are results of delayed in response time and inadequate fire-fighting facilities available. Since buildings are constructed in complex manner and possess enormous risk, risk evaluation is required to ensure the safe design of building and also to assess the fire protection system installed in building. Forwards, Fire risk assessment is mandatorily required assessing the fire outbreaks that may occur and knowledge of possible social, economic and ecologic consequence from there. The efforts needs to be made to reduce the chances of occurrence of fire or fire spread. The awareness towards the fire safety rules and models may reduce the disasters caused due to fire or its control. Literature suggests framework and models to improve the fire safety in the automation of buildings and disaster prone areas. Literature also suggested the importance of embedded system in the fire safety environment systems. Scientists and engineers are working to improve the efficiency and accuracy of existing methods of fire detections. Authors have suggested a number of improvements in terms of simulation or experiment set. Utilisation of embedded system with sensors and controllers in fire safety systems made the systems advanced and efficient for performance.

REFERENCES

[1] Berry, Dave, et al. *"FireGrid: Integrated emergency response and fire safety engineering for the future built environment."* UK e-Science Programme All Hands Meeting, 2005.

[2] Leveson, Nancy. "A new accident model for engineering safer systems." *Safety science* 42.4 (2004): 237-270.

[3] Novak, Thomas, and Andreas Gerstinger. "Safety-and security-critical services in building automation and control systems." *IEEE Transactions on industrial electronics* 57.11 (2010): 3614-3621.

[4] XU, Zhi, et al. "Fire Detection Algorithm Based on Embedded System Using Infrared Pictures [J]." *Science Technology and Engineering* 1 (2008): 024.

[5] Cheung, Sai On, Kevin KW Cheung, and Henry CH Suen. "CSHM: Web-based safety and health monitoring system for construction management." *Journal of Safety Research* 35.2 (2004): 159-170.

[6] Zhang, Sijie, et al. "Integrating BIM and safety: an automated rule-based checking system for safety planning and simulation." Proceedings of CIB W099 99 (2011): 24-26.

[7] Son, Byungrak, Yong-sork Her, and Jung-Gyu Kim. "A design and implementation of forest-fires surveillance system based on wireless sensor networks for South Korea mountains." *International Journal of Computer Science and Network Security (IJCSNS)* 6.9 (2006): 124-130.

[8]   Bonfiglio, Annalisa, et al. "Emergency and work." *Wearable Monitoring Systems*. Springer US, 2011. 205-219.

[9]   Hartung, Carl, et al. "FireWxNet: A multi-tiered portable wireless system for monitoring weather conditions in wildland fire environments." *Proceedings of the 4th international conference on Mobile systems, applications and services*. ACM, 2006.

[10]   Kiritsis, Dimitris, Ahmed Bufardi, and Paul Xirouchakis. "Research issues on product lifecycle management and information tracking using smart embedded systems" *Advanced Engineering Informatics* 17.3 (2003): 189-202.

[11]   Mohamed, Sherif. "Safety climate in construction site environments." *Journal of construction engineering and management* 128.5 (2002): 375-384.

[12]   CHEN, Xiao-juan, Le-ping BU, and Qi-xiu LI. "A fire-detection method based on image processing technique [J]." *Journal of Naval University of Engineering* 3 (2007): 002.

[13]   Kaiser, Bernhard, Catharina Gramlich, and Marc Förster. "State/event fault trees—A safety analysis model for software-controlled systems." *Reliability Engineering & System Safety* 92.11 (2007): 1521-1537.

[14]   Yang, K. T. "Role of fire field models as a design tool for performance-based fire-code implementation." *International Journal on Engineering Performance-Based Fire Codes* 1.1 (1999): 11-17.

[15]   Dietrich, Dietmar, et al. "Communication and computation in buildings: A short introduction and overview." *IEEE transactions on industrial electronics* 57.11 (2010): 3577-3584.

[16]   Sun, Qi-bo, et al. "Internet of Things: Summarize on Concepts, Architecture and Key Technology Problem [J]." *Journal of Beijing University of Posts and Telecommunications* 3.3 (2010): 1-9.

[17]   Ramya, V., and B. Palaniappan. "Embedded system for Hazardous Gas detection and Alerting." *International Journal of Distributed and Parallel Systems (IJDPS)* Vol 3 (2012): 287-300.

[18]   Novak, Thomas, Albert Treytl, and Peter Palensky. "Common approach to functional safety and system security in building automation and control systems." *2007 IEEE Conference on*

Emerging Technologies and Factory Automation (EFTA 2007). IEEE, 2007.

[19] Nazier, Ramy, and Thomas Bauer. "Automated risk-based testing by integrating safety analysis information into system behavior models." Software Reliability Engineering Workshops (ISSREW), 2012 *IEEE 23rd International Symposium on. IEEE*, 2012.

[20] Kriaa, Siwar, et al. "A survey of approaches combining safety and security for industrial control systems." *Reliability Engineering & System Safety* 139 (2015): 156-178.

[21] Hannan, M. A., et al. "Development of an embedded vehicle safety system for frontal crash detection." *International Journal of Crashworthiness* 13.5 (2008): 579-587.

[22] Ramya, V., B. Palaniappan, and K. Karthick. "Embedded controller for vehicle In-Front obstacle detection and cabin safety alert system." *International Journal of Computer Science & Information Technology* 4.2 (2012): 117.

[23] Qinqin, Chen, et al. "Environmental risk source management system for the petrochemical industry." *Process Safety and Environmental Protection* 92.3 (2014): 251-260.

[24] Priya, K. Padma, et al. "Smart Gas Cylinder Using Embedded System." *International Journal of Innovative Research in Electrical, Electronics, Instrumentation and Control Engineering (IJIREEICE)* Vol 2 (2014): 958-962.

[25] Zhao, Ling, et al. "Design of Forest Fire Monitoring System based on Wireless Sensor Networks [J]." *Journal of Chongqing Institute of Technology (Natural Science)* 2 (2009): 036.

[26] Reza Akhondi, Mohammad, et al. "Applications of wireless sensor networks in the oil, gas and resources industries." 2010 *24th IEEE International Conference on Advanced Information Networking and Applications*. IEEE, 2010.

[27] Panesar-Walawege, Rajwinder Kaur, Mehrdad Sabetzadeh, and Lionel Briand. "A model-driven engineering approach to support the verification of compliance to safety standards." 2011 *IEEE 22nd*

152   *Rajesh Singh, Anita Gehlot, Rohit Samkaria et al.*

International Symposium on Software Reliability Engineering. IEEE, 2011.

[28] Acharyulu, PV Srinivas, and P. Seetharamaiah. "A framework for safety automation of safety-critical systems operations." *Safety Science* 77 (2015): 133-142.

[29] Zeng, Yuanyuan, et al. *"Building fire emergency detection and response using wireless sensor networks."* (2009).

[30] Sahulhameed, K., et al. "Artificial eye and sensory based an intelligent robot for fire extinguishment task." *Int. J. Adv. Comp. Theory Engg* 2.1 (2013): 101-105.

[31] Sadvandi, Sara, Nicolas Chapon, and Ludovic Pietre-Cambacédes. "Safety and security interdependencies in complex systems and sos: Challenges and perspectives." *Complex Systems Design & Management*. Springer Berlin Heidelberg, 2012. 229-241.

[32] Feo-Arenis, Sergio, et al. "The Wireless fire alarm system: Ensuring conformance to industrial standards through formal verification." *International Symposium on Formal Methods*. Springer International Publishing, 2014.

[33] Xueli, Chen, Ci Wenyan, and Cai Suhua. "Notice of Retraction Role of wireless sensor networks in forest fire prevention." *Computer Engineering and Technology (ICCET),* 2010 2nd International Conference on. Vol. 4. IEEE, 2010.

[34] Lehto, Mark R., Mary F. Lesch, and William J. Horrey. "Safety warnings for automation." *Springer handbook of automation*. Springer Berlin Heidelberg, 2009. 671-695.

[35] Bhattacharjee, Sudipta, et al. "Wireless sensor network-based fire detection, alarming, monitoring and prevention system for Bord-and-Pillar coal mines." *Journal of Systems and Software* 85.3 (2012): 571-581.

[36] Yoon, Ik Keun, et al. "A Practical Framework for Mandatory Job Safety Analysis Embedded in the Permit-to-Work System and Application to Gas Industry." *Journal of Chemical Engineering of Japan* 44.12 (2011): 976-988.

[37] Kumaran, S., and R. Raja Mohan. "Fire Control in Industries using Controller Area Network." i-Manager's *Journal on Instrumentation & Control Engineering* 1.1 (2012): 32.

[38] Martin, Helmut, et al. "Functional Safety of Automated Driving Systems: Does ISO 26262 Meet the Challenges?." *Automated Driving*. Springer International Publishing, 2017. 387-416.

[39] Obirailo, Oxana. *"Challenges of SAS (Safety Automation System) execution."* (2014).

[40] Ahmad, Azwin Hazrina, et al. "A Study on Intelligent System for Fire Rescue Operation." *Advanced Science Letters* 20.1 (2014): 3-7.

[41] Ho, Chao-Ching, Ming-Chen Chen, and Tsung-Ting Tsai. "Development of Sensory Fusion-Based Intelligent Fire Fighting Robot." *Advanced Science Letters* 4.6-7 (2011): 2037-2042.

[42] Li, Linguo, Hui Liu, and Shujing Li. "Intelligent Fire Monitoring System Based on the Information Fusion Algorithm." *Sensor Letters* 14.11 (2016): 1094-1098.

[43] De Rademaeker, Eddy, et al. "A review of the past, present and future of the European loss prevention and safety promotion in the process industries." *Process Safety and Environmental Protection* 92.4 (2014): 280-291.

[44] Babur, Ferhat, Emre Cevikcan, and M. Bulent Durmusoglu. "Axiomatic Design for Lean-oriented Occupational Health and Safety systems: An application in shipbuilding industry." *Computers & Industrial Engineering* 100 (2016): 88-109.

[45] Singh, Rajesh, and Shailesh Mishra. "Temperature monitoring in wireless sensor network using Zigbee transceiver module." *Power, Control and Embedded Systems (ICPCES),* 2010 International Conference on. IEEE, 2010.

[46] Singh, Rajesh, Shailesh Mishra, and Pankaj Joshi. "Pressure monitoring in wireless sensor network using Zigbee transceiver module." *Computer and Communication Technology (ICCCT),* 2011 2nd International Conference on. IEEE, 2011.

[47] Meera, C. S., et al. "Implementation of an incampus fire alarm system using ZigBee." *Computing for Sustainable Global Development (INDIACom),* 2015 2nd International Conference on. IEEE, 2015.

[48] Teja, GNL Ravi, et al. "Land slide detection and monitoring system using wireless sensor networks (wsn)." *Advance Computing Conference (IACC),* 2014 IEEE International. IEEE, 2014.

[49] Mishra, Manish Kumar, Rajesh Singh, and Rohit Samkaria. "WPAN-Based Energy Efficient Automation System for Buildings." *Proceeding of International Conference on Intelligent Communication,* Control and Devices. Springer Singapore, 2017.

[50] Agarwal, Aditya, et al. "A Design and Application of Forest Fire Detection and Surveillance System Based on GSM and RF Modules." *Proceeding of International Conference on Intelligent Communication, Control and Devices.* Springer Singapore, 2017.

[51] Sharma, Sajal, et al. "UAV for Surveillance and Environmental Monitoring." *Indian Journal of Science and Technology* 9.43 (2016).

[52] Shukla, Abhinav, Rajesh Singh, and Anita Gehlot. "In-campus Generator-Substation Monitoring and Control Using LabVIEW." *Proceeding of International Conference on Intelligent Communication, Control and Devices.* Springer Singapore, 2017.

[53] Gupta, Tanisha, et al. "Design and Development of Low-Cost Wireless Parameter Monitoring System for Nuclear Power Plant." *Proceeding of International Conference on Intelligent Communication, Control and Devices.* Springer Singapore, 2017.

[54] Moreno, M. Victoria, José Luis Hernández Ramos, and Antonio F. Skarmeta. "User role in IoT-based systems." *Internet of Things (WF-IoT),* 2014 IEEE World Forum on. IEEE, 2014.

[55] Sung, Wen-Tsai, and Yao-Chi Hsu. "Designing an industrial real-time measurement and monitoring system based on embedded system and ZigBee." *Expert Systems with Applications* 38.4 (2011): 4522-4529.

[56] Upadhyay, Rochan, et al. *"An architecture for an integrated fire emergency response system for the built environment."* (2008).

[57] San-Miguel-Ayanz, Jesus, and Nicolas Ravail. "Active fire detection for fire emergency management: Potential and limitations for the

operational use of remote sensing." *Natural Hazards* 35.3 (2005): 361-376.

[58] Gwynne, S., et al. "Modelling occupant interaction with fire conditions using the building EXODUS evacuation model." *Fire Safety Journal* 36.4 (2001): 327-357.

[59] Brailsford, Sally C., et al. "Emergency and on-demand health care: modelling a large complex system." *Journal of the Operational Research Society* 55.1 (2004): 34-42.

[60] Navon, Ronie. "Research in automated measurement of project performance indicators." *Automation in Construction* 16.2 (2007): 176-188.

[61] Birgit Östmana, Daniel Brandonb, Håkan Frantzichc, "Fire safety engineering in timber buildings," *Fire Safety Journal*, 2017.

[62] Søren Madsen, Nis P. Lange, Luisa Giuliani, Grunde Jomaas, Boyan S. Lazarov, Ole Sigmund, "Topology optimization for simplified structural fire safety," *Engineering Structures* 124 (2016) 333–343.

[63] Carlee Lehna, Joy Merrell b, Stephen Furmanek a, Stephanie Twyman, *"Home fire safety intervention pilot with urban older adults living in Wales,"* (2016):4985-4991.

[64] Margrethe Kobes, Ira Helsloo, Baukede Vries, Jos G. Post, "Building safety and human behaviour in fire: A literature review," *Fire Safety Journal* 45(2010):1–11.

[65] Stewart, Robert John, James Schaff, and Paul Hammond. *"Methods and systems for enhancing firearm safety through wireless network monitoring "* U.S. Patent No. 9,658,012. 23 May 2017.

[66] Cheng, Min-Yuan, et al. "BIM integrated smart monitoring technique for building fire prevention and disaster relief." *Automation in Construction* 84 (2017): 14-30.

[67] Croce, Paul, et al. "The International FORUM of Fire Research Directors: A Position Paper on Performance Based Codes and Performance Based Design for Fire Applications." *Fire Safety* Journal (2017).

[68]   Vijayalakshmi, S. R., and S. Muruganand. "Internet of Things technology for fire monitoring system." *Int. Res. J. Eng. Technol* 4.6 (2017): 2140-2147.

[69]   Alam, Md Fasiul, et al. "Augmented and virtual reality based monitoring and safety system: A prototype IoT platform." *Journal of Network and Computer Applications* 89 (2017): 109-119.

[70]   Shinde, Reshma, et al. "Need for Wireless Fire Detection Systems using IOT." *International Research Journal of Engineering and Technology* (2017).

[71]   Novak, Jeremy, et al. "Safety outcomes for engineering asset management organizations: Old problem with new solutions?." *Reliability Engineering & System Safety* 160 (2017): 67-73.

[72]   Ackley, H. Sprague, and Jean-Luc Courtemanche. "*Safety system and method.*" U.S. Patent No. 9,564,035. 7 Feb. 2017.

[73]   Apvrille, Ludovic, and Letitia W. Li. "Safe and Secure Support for Public Safety Networks." *Wireless Public Safety Networks* 3. 2017. 185-210.

[74]   Shakdher, Arjun, and Kavita Pandey. "REDAlert+: Medical/Fire Emergency and Warning System using Android Devices." *International Journal of E-Health and Medical Communications (IJEHMC)* 8.1 (2017): 37-51.

[75]   Tseng, Wei-Wen, et al. "To Improve the Care Environments by Using Fire Safety Engineering for Existing Small-Scale Hospitals in Taiwan." *Fire Science and Technology 2015*. Springer Singapore, 2017. 373-381.

[76]   Bongiovanni, Ivano, et al. "Implementation of best practices for emergency response and recovery at a large hospital: A fire emergency case study." *Safety science* 96 (2017): 121-131.

[77]   Santos-Reyes, Jaime, and Alan N. Beard. "An analysis of the emergency response system of the 1996 Channel tunnel fire." *Tunnelling and Underground Space Technology* 65 (2017): 121-139.

[78]   Piriou, Pierre-Yves, Jean-Marc Faure, and Jean-Jacques Lesage. "Generalized Boolean logic Driven Markov Processes: A powerful modeling framework for Model-Based Safety Analysis of dynamic

repairable and reconfigurable systems." *Reliability Engineering & System Safety* 163 (2017): 57-68.

[79] Magnognou, Brady, et al. "Risk analysis of unburnt gas ignition in an exhaust system connected to a confined and mechanically ventilated enclosure fire." *Fire Safety Journal* (2017).

[80] Van Weyenberge, Bart, et al. "Response surface modelling in quantitative risk analysis for life safety in case of fire." *Fire Safety Journal* (2017).

[81] González-Jorge, H., et al. "Low-Altitude Long-Endurance Solar Unmanned Plane for Forest Fire Prevention: Application to the Natural Park of Serra do Xures (spain)." *ISPRS-International Archives of the Photogrammetry, Remote Sensing and Spatial Information Sciences* (2017): 135-139.

[82] Garcia-Jimenez, Santiago, et al. "Forest fire detection: A fuzzy system approach based on overlap indices." *Applied Soft Computing* 52 (2017): 834-842.

[83] Wu, Jiping, and Yuenian Li. *"Forest fire early-warning system and method based on infrared thermal imaging technology."* U.S. Patent No. 9,666,050. 30 May 2017.

[84] Amanatiadis, Angelos, et al. "Real-time surveillance detection system for medium-altitude long-endurance unmanned aerial vehicles." *Concurrency and Computation: Practice and Experience* (2017).

[85] Filizzola, Carolina, et al. "RST-FIRES, an exportable algorithm for early-fire detection and monitoring: Description, implementation, and field validation in the case of the MSG-SEVIRI sensor." *Remote Sensing of Environment* 192 (2017): e2-e25.

[86] Ye, Shiping, et al. "An effective algorithm to detect both smoke and flame using color and wavelet analysis." *Pattern Recognition and Image Analysis* 27.1 (2017): 131-138.

[87] Hua, Lizhong, and Guofan Shao. "The progress of operational forest fire monitoring with infrared remote sensing." *Journal of Forestry Research* (2017): 1-15.

[88] Pereira, Mário Gonzalez, et al. "Fire on the Hills: An Environmental History of Fires and Fire Policy in Mediterranean-Type Ecosystems."

Environmental History in the Making. Springer International Publishing, 2017. 145-169.

[89]   Chu, Thuan, Xulin Guo, and Kazuo Takeda. "Effects of Burn Severity and Environmental Conditions on Post-Fire Regeneration in Siberian Larch Forest." *Forests* 8.3 (2017): 76.

[90]   Hamadeh, Nizar, et al. "Using correlative data analysis to develop weather index that estimates the risk of forest fires in Lebanon & Mediterranean: Assessment versus prevalent meteorological indices." *Case Studies in Fire Safety* 7 (2017): 8-22.

[91]   Di Giuseppe, Francesca, et al. "*Improving CAMS biomass burning estimations by means of the Global ECMWF Fire Forecast system (GEFF)."* (2017).

[92]   Šturm, Tomaž, and Tomaž Podobnikar. "A probability model for long-term forest fire occurrence in the Karst forest management area of Slovenia." *International Journal of Wildland Fire* 26.5 (2017): 399-412

[93]   Bayne, Karen, Samuel Damesin, and Melissa Evans. "*The internet of things–wireless sensor networks and their application to forestry."* NZ Journal of Forestry 61.4 (2017): 37.

[94]   Cerqueira, Diogo, Filipa Carvalho, and Rui Bettencourt Melo. "Is It Smart to Use Smartphones to Measure Illuminance for Occupational Health and Safety Purposes?." *International Conference on Applied Human Factors and Ergonomics.* Springer, Cham, 2017.

[95]   Bianchini, Augusto, et al. "An innovative methodology for measuring the effective implementation of an Occupational Health and Safety Management System in the European Union." *Safety science* 92 (2017): 26-33.

[96]   Tchiehe, Derrick Nanda, and Francois Gauthier. "Classification of risk acceptability and risk tolerability factors in occupational health and safety." *Safety science* 92 (2017): 138-147.

[97]   Walser, Tobias, Réjane Morand Bourqui, and Christoph Studer. "Combination of life cycle assessment, risk assessment and human biomonitoring to improve regulatory decisions and policy making for

chemicals." *Environmental Impact Assessment Review* 65 (2017): 156-163.

[98] Smith, Meredith Y., et al. "Structured Benefit-Risk Assessment Across the Product Lifecycle: Practical Considerations." *Therapeutic Innovation & Regulatory Science* (2017): 2168479017696272.

[99] Johnson, Randy S. *"Vehicle safety belt bypass warning system."* U.S. Patent No. 9,555,739. 31 Jan. 2017.

[100] Axelsson, Jakob. "Safety in vehicle platooning: A systematic literature review." *IEEE Transactions on Intelligent Transportation Systems* 18.5 (2017): 1033-1045.

[101] Zhao, Ding, et al. "Accelerated evaluation of automated vehicles safety in lane-change scenarios based on importance sampling techniques." *IEEE transactions on intelligent transportation systems* 18.3 (2017): 595-607.

[102] Koopman, Philip, and Michael Wagner. "Autonomous Vehicle Safety: An Interdisciplinary Challenge." *IEEE Intelligent Transportation Systems Magazine* 9.1 (2017): 90-96.

[103] Lybbert, Andrew H., et al. "Reproductive success of wind, generalist, and specialist pollinated plant species following wildfire in desert landscapes." *International Journal of Wildland Fire* 26.12 (2018): 1030-1039.

[104] Costafreda-Aumedes, Sergi, Carles Comas, and Cristina Vega-Garcia. "Human-caused fire occurrence modelling in perspective: a review." *International Journal of Wildland Fire* 26.12 (2018): 983-998.

[105] Gould, J. S., et al. "Comparison of three methods to quantify the fire spread rate in laboratory experiments." *International Journal of Wildland Fire* 26.10 (2017): 877-883.

[106] Nelson, Kellen N., et al. "Simulated fire behaviour in young, postfire lodgepole pine forests." *International Journal of Wildland Fire* 26.10 (2017): 852-865.

In: LoRA and IoT Networks …   ISBN: 978-1-53617-164-8
Editors: A. Gehlot, R. Singh et al.   © 2020 Nova Science Publishers, Inc.

Chapter 7

MOBILE PLATFORM LOCALIZATION IN INDOOR/OUTDOOR TECHNIQUES: A REVIEW

Anita Gehlot[1,*], Rajesh Singh[1,†], Rohit Samakria[2,‡],
S. Choudhury[3,§] and Bhupendra Singh[4]
[1]Lovely Professional University, Jalandhar, India
[2]IIT, Kanpur, India
[3]University of Petroleum and Energy Studies, Dehradun, India
[4]Schematics Microelectronics, Dehradun, India

ABSTRACT

Received Signal Strength Indicator (RSSI) is one of the best-known methods of localization. RSSI is an estimated measure of power level that a RF device receives from an access point. This estimate strength provides a coarse detail about the node localization, to perform the coordination

---
* Corresponding Author's Email: eranita5@gmail.com.
† Corresponding Author's Email: srajssssece@gmail.com.
‡ Corresponding Author's Email: rohit.samkaria93@gmail.com.
§ Corresponding Author's Email: schoudhury@ddn.upes.ac.in.

tasks. This chapter discusses the literature review of RSSI method. RSSI is concluded as an indoor localization approach. In literature, many experimental researches have been carried out by the authors and the results show that the RSSI is much more accurate than the GPS for indoor localization. A comparison has been carried out for the RSSI based systems on the basis of the microcontroller, frequency of operation, memory and communication media. It is concluded that RFID and ZigBee can be combined for better results.

Keywords: robots, Received Signal Strength Indicator, Sonar

INTRODUCTION

The challenging competencies required for a mobile robot is one of the most critical task, like navigation. Navigation need four parameters to work, which inclues perception, localization, cognition and control. With these four competantices, the mobile robot can extract the data from the sensors, can determine its position in the environment, decides how to act in order to achieve its goals and modulates its motor outputs to achieve the trajectory for desired position. The recent research has been focused on these fours components. Figure 1(a) shows the classification of robot localization.

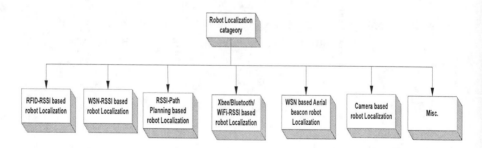

Figure 1(a). Robot Localization classification.

There are two techniques that mostly preferred in the robot localization a) Local Techniques and b) Global Localizations Techniques. The second technique is the most powerful technique because local techniques aims to compensate the odometric error during the navigation and require the initial location. It is not possible to recover local localization techniques, if they lose their track but the global techniques have the capability to localize the position without any prior knowledge of the initial position [75].

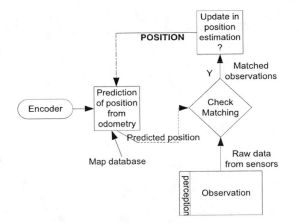

Figure 1(b). General schematic for mobile robot localization.

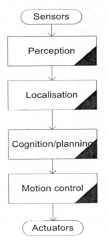

Figure 1(c). An Architecture for Map-based (or model-based) Navigation.

Figure 1(d). An Architecture for Behavior-based Navigation.

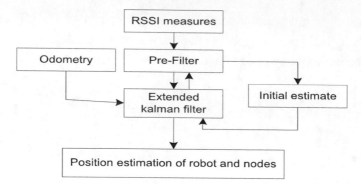

Figure 1(e). SLAM Algorithm with RSSI [7].

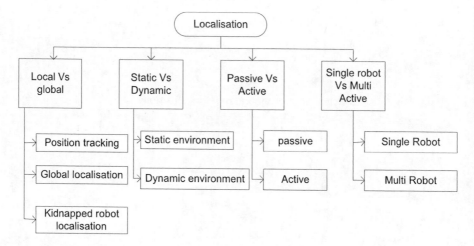

Figure 1(f). Flow chart of Robot Localization.

Shue, Sam et al. (2013) said that the wireless sensor networks are the part of robotics. Localization is associated with the route planning, mapping, and detection [7] as shown in Figure 1(e). The report has recently presented a method for determining the position concerning the nodes regarding the WSN by utilizing the received signal strength as part of the mobile robot and a dispensed technique for location refinement utilizing the standard information flow of the networking [8].

Roberts, James F., et al. (2009) presented a cascaded filtering technique based, custom range and bearing system, which is followed by Radio Frequency (RF) communication [9] as shown in Figure 3 and 4.

Figure 2(b). Research set-up with Mica2 nodes in the parking of the University of Seville. (b) Romeo, the movable robot to communicate with the system. (c): Node placed on Romeo [8].

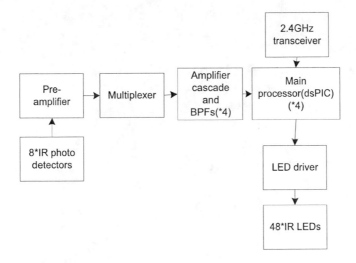

Figure 3. Strategy diagram of RABIT detector for infra-red signal route with RF transceiver [9].

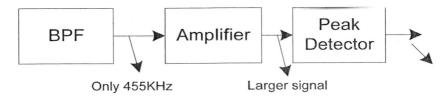

Figure 4. Block diagram of an individual filtration cascade stage with the results [9].

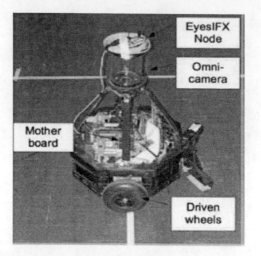

Figure 5(a). The robot and its parts.

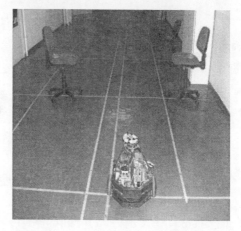

Figure 5(b). The robot and WSN implemented in the experimental environment [10].

Menegatti, Emanuele, et al. (2009) suggested the technique for the localization of the mobile robot whilst at the same time location of node to Wireless Sensor Network (WSN) as part of mapped utilizing one range measurement. Distance of WSN to the closest node is calculated through calculating the RSSI concerning the obtained radio messages using Extended Kalman Filter SLAM algorithm with an error of less than 1m is obtained [10]. Refer Figure 5.

Kothari, Nisarg, et al. (2012) introduced a methodology with the help of smartphone, for indoor localization with incorporating wireless signal strength fingerprinting. A number of participants are utilized to check the process into two separate indoor conditions and reliability for localisation is attained on the order concerning 5m [12]. Refer Figure 6.

Perkins, Chris, et al. (2011) discussed two ways of distance sensing between robots. RSSI doesn't require any additional hardware but Time Difference of Arrival (TDOA) for communication and processing makes use of commercially available wireless sensor. TDOA needs a microphone and sound source. TDOA is found to be superior to RSSI in accuracy. Two techniques concerning distance-only sensing for the limited robotic systems have already been investigated and compared [33]. Refer Figure 7.

Figure 6. RSSI database production using the innovator robot and PF changes. The accepted deviation concerning the PF ripple is ~1m more than the timeframe [12].

Vähä, Pentti, et al. (2013) said that, numerous development operations have fused mechanized hardware, means, and techniques into their general practices. Enhanced sensor advancements and the enhancing usage concerning the creation of information demonstrating (BIM) can provide a new possible outcome towards covering the various requirements and procedures happening all through the constructing life cycle [37]. Cavallo, Filippo, et al. (2014) described the ECHORD experiment ASTROMOBILE and the project aim to test the design and development of the system for successful and upgrading the quality of the life. System consists of mobile platform called ASTRO [43]. Min, Byung-Cheol et al. (2014) described the evolution of a robotic follower system with the ultimate goal of independent convoying for creating end-to-end information. For bearing approximation with directional transmitting aerial, a Centroid Algorithm (WCA) has been hired, which is a technique for active transmitting aerial tracking and direction of appearance (DOA) estimation [44]. A number of techniques to be considered for the machine learning that are the appropriate approach for Autonomous Mobile Robot Localization. By using the partially random tag distribution of the RFID tag, each region in the different environment is uniquely identified [46]. Refer Figure 8.

Figure 7. Two mini-bots using RSSI and omnidirectional TDOA detection [33].

Figure 8. Mobile robot [46].

RFID, RSSI BASED INDOOR ROBOT LOCALIZATION

Deyle, Travis, et al. (2009) suggested an excellent signal (RSSI) for each of the marked issues in possible circumstances. The impact of each pixel in the 'RSSI signal' is calculated for RF sign with a specific label in the comparison method. Faster techniques towards acquiring scanned RFID information, such as electronically reviewed antenna arrays, would definitely have the variety of benefits, incorporating the capability towards handling dynamic conditions as well as creating further estimates off different aspects [2]. Refer Figure 9.

Figure 9. Target location "highlighted" [2].

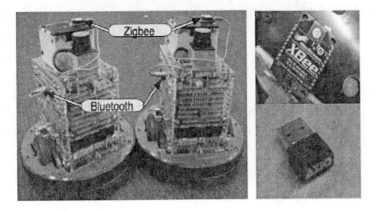

Figure 10. Scarab robots [4].

Fink, Jonathan, et al. (2009) showed the research work of the low-power devices radiates radio signal in environment, with zigbee and bluetooth to obtain a desired result. Here results were presented through the experiment conducted in indoor hallway with the two autonomous robots having radio signal devices connected to them. With the help of radio signal model the RSSI measurements were simulated and they were matched with the experimentally collected RSSI measurements, low-power radio signal devices and predicted RSSI were suggested for robotics application. Refer Figure 10.

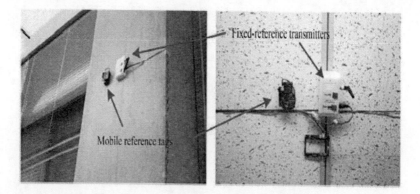

Figure 11. The node set up underneath the roof [5].

Ahn, Hyo-Sung et al. (2009) discussed a method to localize a stationary object in the surrounding place. From a fixed reference node, the RSSI of radio signals were radiated. To generate a precise signal, the node were placed at desired position. As the environment changes, the parameters of signal attenuation were updated from cloud server therefore proposed method was capable of changing the parameter as per changes in environment. Many experiments were carried out to show that the proposed method is much better than a commercial location-based service (LBS) chipset. Refer Figure 11.

Oliveira, Luis, et al. (2014) discussed an anchor-less relative localization algorithm for multi-robots team. Messages were exchanged between nodes for the RSSI readings were collected and localization was performed. Distance is inversely proportional to RSSI between two nodes, communicating to each other. To achieve this, Kalman filtering system and the Floyd–Warshall algorithm were recommended to establish smooth RSSI [6]. Cheng, Long et al. (2011) introduced the major error occured during the localization and how to reduce it with hybrid RSSI/TODA. RSSI is measured with iterative recursive weighted average filter and these measurements were fitted by polynomial model. Accuracy of RSSI localization was improved by proposed method of iterative recursive weighted average filter on the condition of lower computation complexity. Polynomial fitting was used to achieve more accuracy in localization. Indoor location precision requirement was satisfied with the experiment i.e., 0.5m [14] as shown in Figure 12 and 13.

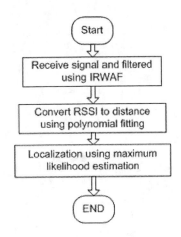

Figure 12. The flow chart of localization [14].

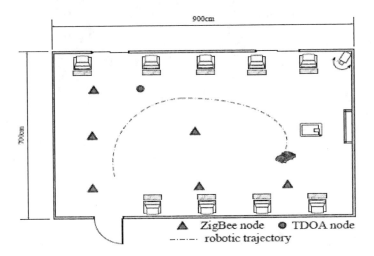

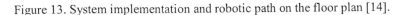

Figure 13. System implementation and robotic path on the floor plan [14].

Figure 14. The (a)RSSI and (b)TDOA nodes and (c) robot [14].

Figure 15. The movable robot PeopleBot with a RFID technique [16].

Cicirelli, Grazia et al. (2012) served the purpose of addressing the development of an autonomous robot by using the passive RFID. Labeling of both valued objects and goal position can be done by passive RFID tags. Moreover, RFID tags can be used by the robot in different navigational purposes in order to keep track of its location. A strategy for the development of an RFID sensor design and a technique for RFID tag localization have been introduced. The design is the blend of an RSSI model (RSSM) and

TDM. The primary contribution involved the learning of the design to describe the connection between tags and antenna. FCM and ANFIS networks have been utilized for understanding the fuzzy inference methods conveying both RSSM and TDM [16]. Refer Figure 15.

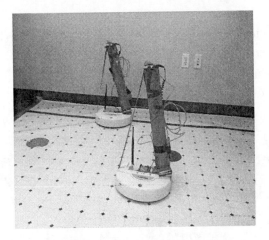

Figure 16. Two LANdroids robots using extra compasses [16].

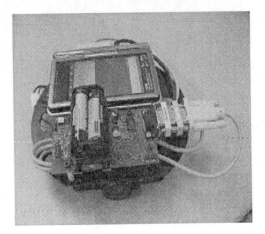

Figure 17. Photograph of a two-wheeled robot [25].

Raghavan, Aswin N., et al. (2010) presented a method to localize a mobile robot with the help of Bluetooth. Hithro limitations were overcomed by a method for distance localization using Bluetooth. The experiment was carried on mobile robot and the error obtained was 0.427 ±0.229m with maximum accuracy. Zickler, Stefan et al. (2010) explained the LANdroid project with a robot, which localizes, tracks, follows other robots or humans, having low ability to sense in an unknown environment. RSSI is mapped with real time implementation and data was obtained. Compass sensor was added to improve the accuracy in localization. [19]. Refer Figure 16.

Malyavej, Veerachai et al. (2013) discussed thelocalization as critical problem for mobile robot. A global positioning system (GPS) is incapable to detect the position for indoor mobile robot. An inertial measurement unit (IMU) can be used for improving the precision and robustness of mobile unit localization. Proposed model work with the help of IMU and WLAN and the method proposed was Kalman filter (EKF) [24]. Ishimoto, Tatsuya et al. (2008) designed a system and common coordinates were given to each robot. A member having no sensor was unable to reach the specified location, in such case wireless communication was used to generate common coordinates. Common coordinates were generated wirelessly for networked robot with RSSI [25]. Refer Figure 17.

Deyle, Travis, et al. (2010) explained that previous robots have LF and HF RFID tags, however now Passive UHF RFID labels are used, which tend to be readable after quite a long distance. These tags enabled the mobile robot to discover them with great ease. These tags are designed with unique ID's with a proper database. This paper presented how a robot can efficiently connect with people around and labeled things [28]. Sun, Pei-Gang, et al. (2007) explained that the existing wireless location technologies issues, including the reliability in range measurement. The localization requirements on RSSI, and provided three ways- Least Square Fitting technique, Signal Strength Distribution technique and Hybrid Location technique were proposed. Research has been conducted to test and analyze the performances and find out that Hybrid Location Method is the best and just needed little bit of computing [29]. Woodman, Oliver et al. (2008) talked about 3 parameters i.e a foot mounted inertial unit, a well elaborated building model, and a particle filter can give precise position. The original issues such as vertical placement, stairways, balance of the surroundings were almost all handled with the assistance of WiFi signal strength [30]. Purohit, Aveek, et al. (2011) explained that the stationary sensor networks tend to not be of much practical utilize, because of the lack of adaptivity as well as minimal coverage. In this paper, controlled-mobile aerial sensor network was discussed for the effective indoor disaster response application [31]. Refer Figure 18.

Figure 18. Experimental setup for determining 2-D space coverage with 4 SensorFly nodes [31].

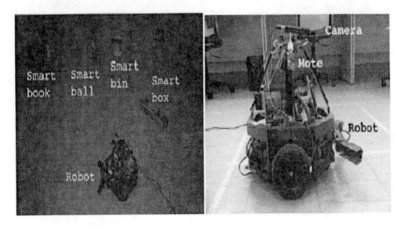

Figure 19. An outline for the experiment setup: that the robot as well as their moveable smart elements and the adjusted Innovator robot system [42].

Pugh, Jim et al. (2008) investigated the issue of little scalable multi robot arrangement control. The automated setup and module were tried in a sensible virtual test system, utilizing standard arrangement sorts and calculations, with and without radio correspondence. The investigations and results were then recreated utilizing the genuine mechanical stage [41]. Menegatti, Emanuele, et al. (2010) displayed an automated framework that adventures Remote Sensor Organize (WSN) advancements for actualizing an encompassing insight situation. The robot finds the items through the radio recurrence correspondence given by the WSN bits. Refer Figure 28. [42].

Figure 20. The omni-directional mobile robot [45].

Wang, Hongbo et al. (2009) discussed a fast self-localization procedure based on ZigBee wireless sensor telegraph and laser sensor, a barrier avoidance algorithm was built on ultrasonic sensor for a mobile robot. To validate the mobile robot and to avoid barriers in real-time, an analytical fuzzy network was established by using heuristic fuzzy rules and Kohonen group of networks [45]. Refer Figure 20.

Sabto, Nosaiba A et al. (2013) said that the Radio Recurrence Distinguishing proof (RFID) innovation can be comprehensively used for enhancing trade. RFID tag can recognize the area position where it dwells; along these lines, a prevalent pattern among analysts is to convey RFID innovation for versatile robot confinement. Since the powers of signs at neighboring areas are like each other, it is a test to utilize a RFID framework as a sensor. The robot detects all milestones in the region to secure the IDs and got flag quality marker (RSSI) estimations of the scattered labels. The robot can find itself contingent upon the arrangement result gave by a nourish forward back-proliferation counterfeit neural system (BPANN) provided with an arrangement of all RSSI estimations read by this robot at a particular area. To be satisfactory, this set ought to just have one high RSSI estimation. The robot detects the area data from a high-esteemed RSSI tag and adds it to a rundown of label IDs alongside the comparing area data. The robot can utilize this data to go between any two recognized areas. The exploratory outcomes exhibit the effectiveness of this proposed framework [46]. Wong, Wallace, et al. (2013) discussed an indoor situating strategy in view of the inertial estimation of the protest and the got flag quality pointer (RSSI) measured from a dynamic RFID tag put on the question and exhibited. The inertial estimation supplements the incorrectness of the RSSI estimations, particularly when the question is far from RFID per user. Analyses demonstrated that the proposed method gives better precision [49]. Loscri, Valeria, et al. (2015) concentrated on the inescapable confinement of target protests in an obscure domain. The ASN depends on the calculation of weights, to "manage" the right course of development, nearer to the objective. RSSI through an ASN was compelling to confine an objective [52]. Yiu, Simon, et al. has studied the Wireless RSSI fingerprint Localization where they examined previous methods and studied the parametric path loss regression model and non-parametric Gaussian Process (GP) and based on these measurements they examined the various aspects such as desnity of access point and impact of an outdated signature map [66]. Warda, Ahmad et al. presented the scanning method for indoor mobile robot using RSSI approach that eliminates the drawback of the congenital finger print which required a time consuming process of creation of database construction. The method compares the column vectors of the kernel matrix and signal strength vector using Euclidean distance matrix [69]. Sequeira, João S et al. described the novel strategy to Radio-Frequency Identification tag detection for human robot interaction. Probalistic algorithm was combined with the anisotropic detection pattern of RFID antenna to obtain a coarse angular position [70]. Du, Jinze et al. proposed the Least Mean Square Method (LMS) that was associated with the trilateration method to estimate the chanel mode parameters for tracking strategy for constrained position localization [72].

WSN, RSSI BASED MOBILE ROBOT LOCALIZATION

Simon, Janos et al. (2011) recommended a WSN protocol with the help of which, their mobile robot routing can be completed for the localization of a movable measurement facility and navigation strategies can also be determined. The SunSPOT nodes (Figure 10) radio communications has an integrated CC2420 radio receiver circuit, works on IEEE 802.15.4 standard with 2.4 GHz to 2.4835 GHz ISM bands [11].

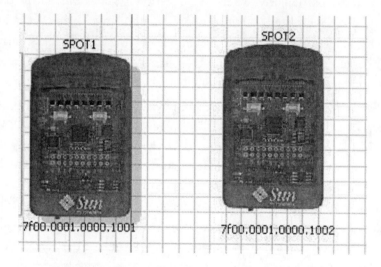

Figure 21. Java based Sun SPOT [11].

Awad, Abdalkarim et al. (2013) explained the most challenging issue in WSN is localization. In the paper different approaches were analyzed and discussed relying on the RSSI. For the estimation of distance two methods were evaluated, the initial method was depending upon analytical techniques and the 2nd on an artificial neural network [13]. Graefenstein, Juergen, et al. (2009) explained the difficulty to determine the physical location of radio nodes in WSN. This paper helped to get the location of mobile robot. An average error of 13cm was determined in the position [15]. No understanding regarding the wireless qualities concerning the stationary nodes are needed. Refer Figure 23.

Figure 22. Impact of surrounding on the wireless transmission [13].

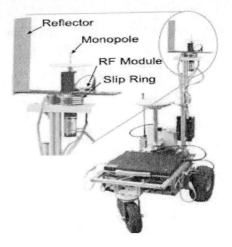

Figure 23. Experimental setup of the robot [15].

Severino, Ricardo (2007) presented a computing application based on WSN technologies. A two- tiered communication is designed for good communication in WSNs. A test-bed application is being designed for validating and performing the theoretical findings [17].

180 *Anita Gehlot, Rajesh Singh, Rohit Samkria et al.*

Figure 24. Indoor environment [17].

Nguyen, Cory Q. et al. (2012) provided the proof of concept for offering a wireless mesh network with wireless services to end customers. This concept also showed the capability to enhance the throughput of the mobile wireless mesh topology system for network traffic to transit data [20]. Refer Figure 25 and 26.

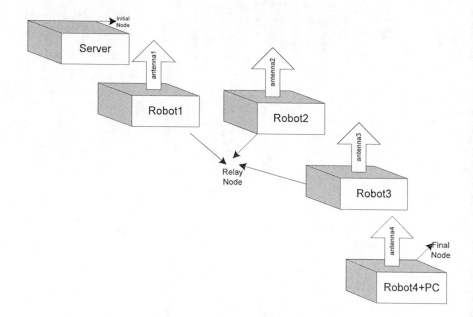

Figure 25. A design utilizing several movable robots holding antennas [20].

Shenoy, Suresh et al. (2005) discussed a method for localization of wireless sensors in hybrid sensor network, where hybrid network consisted of a huge number of sensor and a few of mobile robots. These mobile robots are localized with the help of GPS. The position of mobile robots is known with the help of message sent by them [23]. Faheem, Ahmed et al. (2010 discussed about the estimation technique based on RSSI with IEEE 802.15.4 network. Distance estimator uses packet loss limits and SD to get the best location with minimum distance error [32]. Peng, Chao et al. (2009) discussed various limitation of frameworks created ealier. In this paper properties of latent UHF RFID frameworks has been considered.

Figure 26. Exterior LE stage of experimentation [20].

The restriction utilizes the k-closest neighbor calculation to assess the physical position of the objective tag [35]. Zhou, Nan et al. (2013) discussed the organization of remote sensor (WSN) in new environment which gives the portable robot productive guide of route [39]. Sun, Dali et al. (2008) considered the issue of multi-robot. The memory of these hubs was used for the trading of guide information between various robots. Maps were produced from robot odometry and run gauges. The proposed technique has been widely tried in USARSim, which serves as reason for the Virtual Robots rivalry at RoboCup, and by genuine investigations with a group of portable robots [40]. Shih, Chia-Yen, et al. (2014) presented an appointing cooperative diverse system, which can enhance application context and can get high application. The fusion of mobile robots and wireless sensor networks (WSN's) is a brilliant example for such a combined effort, and many other latest research conclusions have highlighted the benefits of combination of these two technologies [48]. Refer Figure 27.

Yuan, Jing, et al. developed a mobile robot to establish the correlation between the sparsely distributed sensor nodes that were not disconnected. The mobility of the robot provides the stationary and disconnected sensor nodes to be dynamically correlated and connected [63].

Figure 27. (a) The tool testing; (b) Mosquito experimentation; (c) Captured mosquitoes with experiments [48].

RSSI AND PATH PLANNING BASED MOBILE ROBOT

Graefenstein, Juergen et al.(2008) informed about that mobile robot localization with the help of low power IEEE 802.15.4 using RSSI. Particle filter was used to localize precisely. The error of 0.32 was obtained while localizing in real time implementation. Lee, Geunho et al. (2011) presented a low cost practical method for localization. This practical model was presented by observing the bats and was capable to sense over 360 degree. An algorithm was proposed and error of 2.6 cm was obtained in sensing if targets are 100 cm away [22]. Refer Figure 28 and 29.

Chen, Jenhui et al. (2005) shared an effective way to arrange calculation (CPPA) and a correspondence convention for the sensor multi-robot frameworks [26]. Tardioli, Danilo, et al. (2010) discussed an entire framework which incorporates three research viewpoints, considered independently. To accomplish these attributes: a multi-robot movement control system in light of a virtual spring–damper display which counteracts correspondence arrange parts [34]. Wu, Han, et al. (2014) discussed about restriction and arrangement control and considered them the key innovations to accomplish coordination and control of swarm robots [47]. Cavallo, Filippo, et al. (2014) gave an innovative viewpoints to build up the Robot-Time framework that can be demonstrated in a society. The investigation embraces an end-client situated point of view, considering a portion of the primary properties of adequacy: ease of use, demeanor, nervousness, trust and personal satisfaction [51]. Refer Figure 30 and 31.

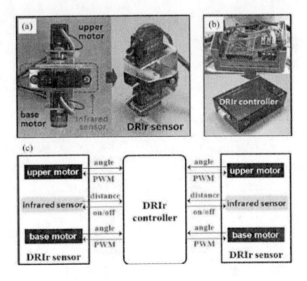

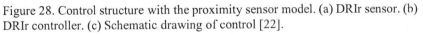

Figure 28. Control structure with the proximity sensor model. (a) DRIr sensor. (b) DRIr controller. (c) Schematic drawing of control [22].

Zhao, Zhongliang, et al. used the WiFi RSSI readings, IMUs and floor plan information into an enhanced practicable filter to achive high accuracy and the tracking algorithms [65]. Zhang, Yunzhou, et al. studied the fluctuation into the RSSI due to various environmental factors that brings adverse effect on the distance measurement and deteriorate the performance of robot localization [68]. Ramiro Martínez-de Dios, José, et al. presented the schemes in which the various anchor nodes in on line learnt the RSSI range models [71].

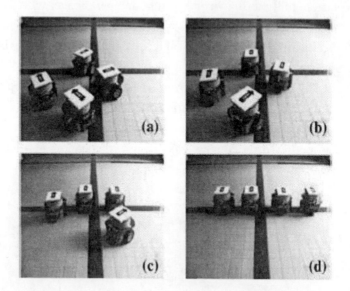

Figure 29. The single row structure generation [22].

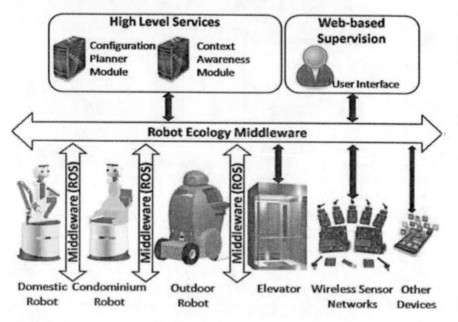

Figure 30. Structure for the Robot-Era technique [51].

Figure 31. Experimental platform [51].

ZIGBEE, BLUETOOTH AND WI-FI, RSSI BASED INDOOR LOCALIZATION

Li, Quanxi et al. (2014) raised the issue of exact area for the portable robot for underground coal mine. Three-point computation of close separation and Gaussian channel was proposed which utilize the established logarithmic separation weakening model [50]. Zàruba, Gergely V., et al. (2007) explained that the sensor utilized for the area estimation. Area evaluations were then processed by utilizing Bayesian separating on test sets inferred by Monte Carlo [38]. Lu, Tien-Fu (2013) discussed a simulation model for the autonomous robot for indoor environment, which contained a gas source emitting chemical concentrations, varing with wind speeds and directions [54].

Galceran, Enric et al. (2013) discussed the coverage path planning of robots. Paper presented the CPP methods, designed in the past and their applications. A brief review for the work was discussed. An experimental set up for exploring CPP was also proposed [55].

Bakdi, Azzeddine, et al. (2017) presented an off line optimal path planning and execution of two-kinect based camera system for indoor robot.

Robot was designed to make use of image processing technique with vision system. A Genetic algorithm based collision avoidance system was designed for indoor environment [56].

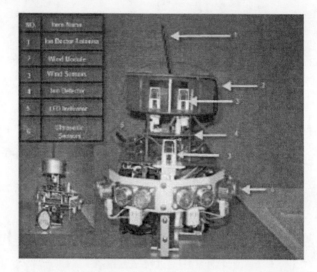

Figure 32. The model of indoor robot [54].

Figure 33. Experimental set up for the leap-frog localization and coverage strategy[55].

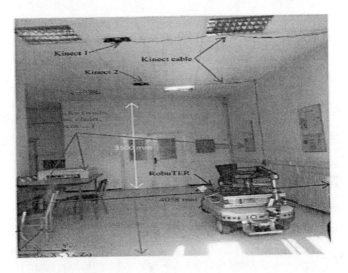

Figure 34. Experimental set up to test the robot [56].

Mac, ThiThoa, et al. (2016) discussed the path learning technique with two different methods namely classical method and heuristic method. The focus of paper was on heuristic based algorithm in robot. The advantages and limitations of each algorithm were also discussed [57]. Canedo-Rodríguez, Adrián et al. proposed a multisensory fusion algorithm to fuse the information provided by the sensors placed on board [60]. Yu et al. studied the key issue for the accuracy that effect the positioning accuracy and optimization of the localization algorithm [73].

WSN BASED ARIEL BEACON ROBOT

Caballero, Fernando, et al. (2008) proposed a technique for 3-D localization involving outdoor wireless sensor network (WSN) simply by utilizing an individual hovering beacon-node on-board of an autonomous helicopter. The method was dependent on particle filtering with no previous information requirement, towards estimation of the location of the node. Figure 35 provided the particle filter for the node location evaluation [1]. The filter utilizes RSSI calculations of the signal obtained from a flying robot functioning as one radio beacon node with GPS DEVICE as part of arrangement to approximate the location.

Figure 35. Experimentation apparatus (a): single node with an antenna (b): The UAV [1].

Maza, Iván, et al. (2011) presented the multi-UAV distributed decisional technology produced as part of the framework for authentic Unmanned Aeronautical Vehicles (UAVs) as well as isolated Sensor Systems (WSNs) [36]. Türkoral, Türker, et al. presented the swarm robotic application for an indoor positioning using standard matrix for Bluetooth and WiFi communication infrastructures [74].

CAMERA BASED ROBOT LOCALIZATION

Shalal, Nagham, et al. presented the orchid mapping and mobile robot localization using on board camera. The system urtilized the tree trunk method for detection and constructing the orchid map using the camera and laser detection fusion [58]. Shalal, Nagham, et al. presented the novel tree trunk detection algorithm to enhance the detection capability by using the camera and scanner data fusion [59]. De San Bernabé et al. proposed a scheme that efficiently exploits the camera measurement and RSSI based target tracking with optimization of the Wireless Camera Network [67].

MISCELLANEOUS

Pathirana, Pubudu N., et al. (2005) displayed the unique strategy for center limitation in a deferral tolerant sensor arrangement (DTN) [3]. Caballero, Fernando, et al. (2008) exhibited the localization in Wireless Sensor Network (WSN) with the help of a robot inside the Network Robotic System (NRS) [8]. Deng-Yin, Zhang et al. (2012) discussed two kinds of localisation algorithm concerning wireless sensor networks for example RSSI localisation protocol on range-based and DV-Hop localisation formula upon free-range technique. When this new combined localization algorithm is simulated, the results came out to be significantly improved [27]. Zaidner, Guy, and Amir Shapiro, a novel data fusion algorithm for low-cost localization and navigation of autonomous vineyard sprayer robots was presented. It helps to reduce the amount of lobour required to perform the task [61]. Vroegindeweij et al. presented the probalistic localization with a practical filter for using inside the poultry houses [62]. Astanin, Sergey, et al. presented a smart vision system for the industrial robotic cell that can recognize and localize a reflective workplace [64].

CONCLUSION

This articleconcludes a review on the localization technology, with good indoor approach. Literature suggests the efficient functioning of RSSI technology and it is more accurate than the GPS for indoor localization. Review have been carried out in many experimental research approaches. A comparative study has been carried out for the different approaches, based on the microcontroller used, frequency of operation, memory and communication media etc. It is concluded that RFID and ZigBee can be combined for efficient functioning of systems and RSSI has the better approach for indoor localization.

REFERENCES

[1] Caballero, Fernando, et al. "A particle filtering method for wireless sensor network localization with an aerial robot beacon." Robotics and Automation, 2008. ICRA 2008. *IEEE International Conference on. IEEE*, 2008.

[2] Deyle, Travis, et al. "Rf vision: Rfid receive signal strength indicator (rssi) images for sensor fusion and mobile manipulation." *2009 IEEE/RSJ International Conference on Intelligent Robots and Systems. IEEE*, 2009.

[3] Pathirana, Pubudu N., et al. "Node localization using mobile robots in delay-tolerant sensor networks." *IEEE Transactions on Mobile Computing 4.3* (2005): 285-296.

[4] Fink, Jonathan, et al. "Experimental characterization of radio signal propagation in indoor environments with application to estimation and control." *2009 IEEE/RSJ International Conference on Intelligent Robots and Systems. IEEE*, 2009.

[5] Ahn, Hyo-Sung, and Wonpil Yu. "Environmental-adaptive RSSI-based indoor localization." *IEEE Transactions on Automation Science and Engineering* 6.4 (2009): 626-633.

[6] Oliveira, Luis, et al. "RSSI-based relative localization for mobile robots." *Ad Hoc Networks* 13 (2014): 321-335.

[7] Shue, Sam, and James M. Conrad. "A survey of robotic applications in wireless sensor networks." Southeastcon, *2013 Proceedings of IEEE. IEEE*, 2013.

[8] Caballero, Fernando, et al. "A probabilistic framework for entire WSN localization using a mobile robot." *Robotics and Autonomous Systems 56.10* (2008): 798-806.

[9] Roberts, James F., et al. "2.5 D infrared range and bearing system for collective robotics." 2009 *IEEE/RSJ International Conference on Intelligent Robots and Systems. IEEE*, 2009.

[10] Menegatti, Emanuele, et al. "Range-only SLAM with a mobile robot and a wireless sensor networks." Robotics and Automation, 2009. ICRA'09. *IEEE International Conference on. IEEE*, 2009.

[11] Simon, Janos, and GoranMartinovic. "Navigation of Mobile Robots Using WSN's RSSI Parameter and Potential Field Method." *Acta Polytechnica Hungarica* 10.4 (2013): 107-118.

[12] Kothari, Nisarg, et al. "Robust indoor localization on a commercial smart phone." *Procedia Computer Science* 10 (2012): 1114-1120.

[13] Awad, Abdalkarim, Thorsten Frunzke, and Falko Dressler. "Adaptive distance estimation and localization in WSN using RSSI measures." Digital System Design Architectures, Methods and Tools, 2007. DSD 2007. *10th Euromicro Conference on. IEEE*, 2007.

[14] Cheng, Long, Cheng-Dong Wu, and Yun-Zhou Zhang. "Indoor robot localization based on wireless sensor networks." *IEEE Transactions on Consumer Electronics* 57.3 (2011): 1099-1104.

[15] Graefenstein, Juergen, et al. "Wireless node localization based on RSSI using a rotating antenna on a mobile robot." Positioning, Navigation and Communication, 2009. *WPNC 2009. 6th Workshop on. IEEE*, 2009.

[16] Cicirelli, Grazia, Annalisa Milella, and Donato Di Paola. "RFID tag localization by using adaptive neuro-fuzzy inference for mobile robot applications." *Industrial Robot: An International Journal* 39.4 (2012): 340-348.

[17] Severino, Ricardo, and Mairio Alves. "Engineering a search and rescue application with a wireless sensor network-based localization mechanism."*2007 IEEE International Symposium on a World of Wireless, Mobile and Multimedia Networks*. IEEE, 2007.

[18] Raghavan, Aswin N., et al. "Accurate mobile robot localization in indoor environments using bluetooth." Robotics and Automation (ICRA), *2010 IEEE International Conference on. IEEE*, 2010.

[19] Zickler, Stefan, and Manuela Veloso. "RSS-based relative localization and tethering for moving robots in unknown environments." Robotics and Automation (ICRA), *2010 IEEE International Conference on. IEEE*, 2010.

[20] Nguyen, Cory Q., et al. "Using mobile robots to establish mobile wireless mesh networks and increase network throughput." *International Journal of Distributed Sensor Networks* 2012 (2012).

[21] Graefenstein, Juergen, and M. Essayed Bouzouraa. "Robust method for outdoor localization of a mobile robot using received signal strength in low power wireless networks." Robotics and Automation, 2008. ICRA 2008. *IEEE International Conference on. IEEE*, 2008.

[22] Lee, Geunho, and Nak Young Chong. "Low-cost dual rotating infrared sensor for mobile robot swarm applications." *IEEE Transactions on Industrial Informatics 7.2* (2011): 277-286.

[23] Shenoy, Suresh, and Jindong Tan. "Simultaneous localization and mobile robot navigation in a hybrid sensor network." *2005 IEEE/RSJ International Conference on Intelligent Robots and Systems. IEEE*, 2005.

[24] Malyavej, Veerachai, WaraponKumkeaw, and ManopAorpimai. "Indoor robot localization by RSSI/IMU sensor fusion." Electrical Engineering/Electronics, Computer, Telecommunications and Information Technology (ECTI-CON), *2013 10th International Conference on. IEEE*, 2013.

[25] Ishimoto, Tatsuya, and Shinsuke Hara. "Use of RSSI for motion control of wirelessly networked robot swarm." Robotic and Sensors Environments, 2008. *ROSE 2008. International Workshop on. IEEE*, 2008.

[26] Chen, Jenhui, and Li-Ren Li. "Path planning protocol for collaborative multi-robot systems." *2005 International Symposium on Computational Intelligence in Robotics and Automation. IEEE*, 2005.

[27] Deng-Yin, Zhang, and Cui Guo-Dong. "A union node localization algorithm based on RSSI and DV-Hop for WSNs." Instrumentation, Measurement, Computer, Communication and Control (IMCCC), *2012 Second International Conference on. IEEE*, 2012.

[28] Deyle, Travis, et al. "*RFID-guided robots for pervasive automation.*" (2010).

[29] Sun, Pei-Gang, et al. "Research on RSSI-based location in smart space."*Acta Electronica Sinica* 35.7 (2007): 1340.

[30] Woodman, Oliver, and Robert Harle. "Pedestrian localisation for indoor environments." *Proceedings of the 10th international conference on Ubiquitous computing. ACM*, 2008.

[31] Purohit, Aveek, et al. "SensorFly: Controlled-mobile sensing platform for indoor emergency response applications." *Information Processing in Sensor Networks (IPSN), 2011 10th International Conference on. IEEE,* 2011.

[32] Faheem, Ahmed, ReinoVirrankoski, and Mohammed Elmusrati. "Improving RSSI based distance estimation for 802.15. 4 wireless sensor networks."Wireless Information Technology and Systems (ICWITS), *2010 IEEE International Conference on. IEEE,* 2010.

[33] Perkins, Chris, et al. "Distance sensing for mini-robots: RSSI vs. TDOA." *2011 IEEE International Symposium of Circuits and Systems (ISCAS). IEEE,* 2011.

[34] Tardioli, Danilo, et al. "Enforcing network connectivity in robot team missions." *The International Journal of Robotics Research* (2010).

[35] Peng, Chao, Max Q-H. Meng, and Huawei Liang. "An experimental system of mobile robot's self-localization based on WSN." 2009 *IEEE International Conference on Automation and Logistics. IEEE,* 2009.

[36] Maza, Iván, et al. "Experimental results in multi-UAV coordination for disaster management and civil security applications." *Journal of intelligent & robotic systems* 61.1-4 (2011): 563-585.

[37] Vähä, Pentti, et al. "Extending automation of building construction— Survey on potential sensor technologies and robotic applications." *Automation in Construction* 36 (2013): 168-178.

[38] Zàruba, Gergely V., et al. "Indoor location tracking using RSSI readings from a single Wi-Fi access point." *Wireless networks* 13.2 (2007): 221-235.

[39] Zhou, Nan, Xiaoguang Zhao, and Min Tan. "RSSI-based mobile robot navigation in grid-pattern wireless sensor network." *Chinese Automation Congress (CAC), 2013. IEEE,* 2013.

[40] Sun, Dali, Alexander Kleiner, and Thomas M. Wendt. "Multi-robot range-only slam by active sensor nodes for urban search and rescue." *Robot Soccer World Cup.* Springer Berlin Heidelberg, 2008.

[41] Pugh, Jim, and AlcherioMartinoli. "Small-scale robot formation movement using a simple on-board relative positioning system." *Experimental Robotics.* Springer Berlin Heidelberg, 2008.

[42] Menegatti, Emanuele, et al. "Discovery, localization and recognition of smart objects by a mobile robot." *International Conference on Simulation, Modeling, and Programming for Autonomous Robots.* Springer Berlin Heidelberg, 2010.

[43] Cavallo, Filippo, et al. "Improving domiciliary robotic services by integrating the ASTRO robot in an AmI infrastructure." *Gearing Up and Accelerating Cross-fertilization between Academic and Industrial Robotics Research in Europe*: Springer International Publishing, 2014. 267-282.

[44] Min, Byung-Cheol, and Eric T. Matson. "Robotic follower system using bearing-only tracking with directional antennas." *Robot Intelligence Technology and Applications 2.* Springer International Publishing, 2014. 37-58.

[45] Wang, Hongbo, Ke Yu, and Bingyi Mao. "Self-localization and obstacle avoidance for a mobile robot." *Neural Computing and Applications* 18.5 (2009): 495-506.

[46] Sabto, Nosaiba A., and Khalid Al Mutib. "Autonomous mobile robot localization based on RSSI measurements using an RFID sensor and neural network BPANN." *Journal of King Saud University-Computer and Information Sciences* 25.2 (2013): 137-143.

[47] Wu, Han, et al. "Precise localization and formation control of swarm robots via wireless sensor networks." *Mathematical Problems in Engineering* 2014 (2014).

[48] Shih, Chia-Yen, et al. "On the cooperation between mobile robots and wireless sensor networks." *Cooperative Robots and Sensor Networks 2014.* Springer Berlin Heidelberg, 2014. 67-86.

[49] Wong, Wallace, et al. "Accurate indoor positioning technique using RSSI assisted inertial measurement." *Future Information Communication Technology and Applications.* Springer Netherlands, 2013. 121-129.

[50] Li, Quanxi, and Lili Wu. "Mobile robot localization in coal mine based on Zigbee." *Mechatronics and Automatic Control Systems.* Springer International Publishing, 2014. 411-418.

[51] Cavallo, Filippo, et al. "Development of a socially believable multi-robot solution from town to home." *Cognitive Computation* 6.4 (2014): 954-967.

[52] Loscri, Valeria, et al. "Associative Search Network for RSSI-based Target Localization in Unknown Environments." *International Conference on Ad Hoc Networks*. Springer International Publishing, 2015.

[53] Cicirelli, Grazia, Annalisa Milella, and Donato Di Paola. *RFID sensor modeling by using an autonomous mobile robot*. INTECH Open Access Publisher, 2011.

[54] Lu, Tien-Fu. "Indoor odour source localisation using robot: Initial location and surge distance matter." *Robotics and Autonomous Systems* 61.6 (2013): 637-647.

[55] Galceran, Enric, and Marc Carreras. "A survey on coverage path planning for robotics." *Robotics and Autonomous Systems* 61.12 (2013): 1258-1276.

[56] Bakdi, Azzeddine, et al. "Optimal path planning and execution for mobile robots using genetic algorithm and adaptive fuzzy-logic control." *Robotics and Autonomous Systems* 89 (2017): 95-109.

[57] Mac, ThiThoa, et al. "Heuristic approaches in robot path planning: A survey." *Robotics and Autonomous Systems* 86 (2016): 13-28.

[58] Shalal, Nagham, et al. "Orchard mapping and mobile robot localisation using on-board camera and laser scanner data fusion–Part B: Mapping and localisation." *Computers and Electronics in Agriculture* 119 (2015): 267-278.

[59] Shalal, Nagham, et al. "Orchard mapping and mobile robot localisation using on-board camera and laser scanner data fusion–Part A: Tree detection." *Computers and Electronics in Agriculture* 119 (2015): 254-266.

[60] Canedo-Rodríguez, Adrián, et al. "Particle filter robot localisation through robust fusion of laser, WiFi, compass, and a network of external cameras." *Information Fusion* 27 (2016): 170-188.

[61] Zaidner, Guy, and Amir Shapiro. "A novel data fusion algorithm for low-cost localisation and navigation of autonomous vineyard sprayer robots." *Biosystems Engineering* 146 (2016): 133-148.

[62] Vroegindeweij, Bastiaan A., JorisIJsselmuiden, and Eldert J. van Henten. "Probabilistic localisation in repetitive environments: Estimating a robot's position in an aviary poultry house." *Computers and Electronics in Agriculture* 124 (2016): 303-317.

[63] Yuan, Jing, et al. "Cooperative localization for disconnected sensor networks and a mobile robot in friendly environments." *Information Fusion* 37 (2017): 22-36.

[64] Astanin, Sergey, et al. "Reflective workpiece detection and localization for flexible robotic cells." *Robotics and Computer-Integrated Manufacturing* 44 (2017): 190-198.

[65] Zhao, Zhongliang, et al. "A real-time robust indoor tracking system in smartphones." *Computer communications* (2017).

[66] Yiu, Simon, et al. "Wireless RSSI fingerprinting localization." *Signal Processing* 131 (2017): 235-244.

[67] de San Bernabé, Alberto, J. R. Martinez-de Dios, and AníbalOllero. "Efficient integration of RSSI for tracking using Wireless Camera Networks." *Information Fusion* 36 (2017): 296-312.

[68] Zhang, Yunzhou, et al. "Particle swarm optimization–based minimum residual algorithm for mobile robot localization in indoor environment." *International Journal of Advanced Robotic Systems* 14.5 (2017): 1729881417729277.

[69] Warda, Ahmad, BojanaPetković, and HannesToepfer. "Scanning method for indoor localization using the RSSI approach." *Journal of Sensors and Sensor Systems* 6.1 (2017): 247.

[70] Sequeira, João S., and Duarte Gameiro. "A Probabilistic Approach to RFID-Based Localization for Human-Robot Interaction in Social Robotics." *Electronics* 6.2 (2017): 32.

[71] Ramiro Martínez-de Dios, José, et al. "On-Line RSSI-Range Model Learning for Target Localization and Tracking." *Journal of Sensor and Actuator Networks* 6.3 (2017): 15.

[72] Du, Jinze, Jean-François Diouris, and Yide Wang. "A RSSI-based parameter tracking strategy for constrained position localization." *EURASIP Journal on Advances in Signal Processing* 2017.1 (2017): 77.

[73] Yu, Zong-zuo, and Gai-zhiGuo. "Improvement of positioning technology based on RSSI in ZigBee networks." *Wireless Personal Communications* 95.3 (2017): 1943-1962.

[74] Türkoral, Türker, et al. "Indoor Localization for Swarm Robotics with Communication Metrics Without Initial Position Information." *Mechatronics and Robotics Engineering for Advanced and Intelligent Manufacturing*. Springer International Publishing, 2017. 207-215.

[75] Silva, Joao, Nuno Lau, and António JR Neves. "Localization techniques for autonomous mobile robots." *Electrónica e Telecomunicações* 5.3 (2011): 309-316.

In: LoRA and IoT Networks ...   ISBN: 978-1-53617-164-8
Editors: A. Gehlot, R. Singh et al.   © 2020 Nova Science Publishers, Inc.

Chapter 8

SMART WATER MANAGEMENT SYSTEM USING PI

Rishi Bajpai[*]

ECE, Lovely Professional University, Phagwara, Punjab, India

ABSTRACT

The major problem while analyzing a large water body or water pipe is to measure the depth and flow of water. In real-time, a person cannot calculate both the parameters with maximum accuracy as well as come up with fast results. So I came up with the solution in which the water flow rate is calculated using the ultrasonic sensor and flow sensor. These sensors give information about the water flow rate and depth of water level. These are attached to the raspberry pi, LCD which measure and display the values in real-time. The cloud server is then updated. Data can be used for analysis and in calculations of chlorine or other chemicals for water treatment. The device could also be employed to calculate the rate and depth of any other liquid. It is also useful in places where there is a requirement of determining the rate of flow and increase of liquid level. For example, apart from manual surveillance in the region where there are chances of flood in a river or water body, we can make the supervision more precise and

---

[*] Corresponding Author's Email: imrishibajpai@gmail.com.

efficient by deploying the device node at that coordinate of the region. It will reduce the chances of human error and can be proved useful in the foundation of intelligent cities.

Keywords: Water Management, Volume Analysis, Raspberry Pi, Ultrasonic Sensor

LITERATURE REVIEW

Water quality is measured and managed by taking samples of water at water storage tanks and then calculating the amount of water level. It consumes time and workforce if we do it manually. The standard mentions the acceptable limit and indicates its background needs. It should be under the critical proposed limit. Due to the absence of an alternative, analyzed data values, over the advisable limit are consumed, which poses a serious issue to life across the globe.

The water is among the very basic needs of human beings. An average healthy individual needs eight glasses of water daily for its body. It is immensely helpful in tasks like providing necessary nutrients and in regulating the temperature of the human body as well as it plays an integral part in the circulation of the vital nutrients inside the body from one part of the body to another. We have employed a node at the starting end of the small-pipe water distribution network channel so that we can improve the quality of water from the very starting point of the network chain. The quality of water in the small-pipe water distribution network chain is managed and controlled based on the signals received from the water quality monitors or the nodes installed at the base point [1].

Due to the daily increase in the population and economy development trend across the biosphere, the existing techniques and methods of water-standard assurance and supervision are far from the satisfactory level. The industries, as well as nations, are exploiting water in large quantities for its welfare, so it becomes the need of the hour to treat the water such that it can be equally qualified for the consumption of the individual. To increase unceasing stability and life of water-standards-supervision systems, depth exploration of the resulting blockages and the appropriate relieve providing methodologies are preferred. A vast number of water management associated approaches uses, and strategy thoughts were tested and gone thoroughly. Different angles of maintainable water-standard management in the twenty-first century were examined, which demonstrated many challenging domains for increased research struggles, including concerns like data accessibility and trustworthiness of data, various issues in complex systems and validity of the methodology, restrictions of computer techniques and procedures, practicality of investigation outputs, concerns while strategy execution, and requirement of exercise programs [2]. Internet, the invention of the millennium, has reconstructed the globe and brought people closer to each other than previous. The daily revolutions in the technologies of computing techniques and communication have brought up the following level of the Internet, the Internet of Things (IoT). As there is an increase in the number of peoples in the world and urban movement going across the world, the cities must convert themselves to the Smart Cities, which can only achieve with the assistance of the Internet of Things in our hands. Water is one of the necessary resources for the sustainable presence of human life, so Smart water management plays a significant role in the smart city concept [3].

Artificial neural networks provide primary information about hydrology. So, it is useful in providing information about elements mixed in water [4].

Many of the nations use the smart water treatment plant as it is safer due to its less interference of livelihood near the water treatment plant. Many countries also show interest in developing these kinds of the smart water treatment plant. However, most of them still tend to use programmable logic controllers-PLCs. Raspberry Pi, also known as a minicomputer that can control the systems associated with it, and it also has advantages like low cost and compact size [5].

In Whatcom County, Washington, increased concentrations of nitrate in ground-level water were of greatest worry. Whatcom County is known and famous for its enormous activities related to agriculture, the majority of which are intensive dairy farm industries. The previous history of concentration of nitrate statistics from 1990 to 2000 was analyzed and processed from different organizations and clubbed into an individual central compound database. A method for collecting geographical information was used to evaluate the spatial and chronological variations in the nitrogen data at a place. The investigation was accompanied in the full locality as well as for individual watersheds and various categories of land usage. Furthermore, nitrate concentration variations with descriptive constraints were also noted, such as depth of sampling, recharge of groundwater, oxygen dissolved in the water, and nitrogen present on the ground loadings was also examined. The result of the investigation displayed that the localities with concentrations levels of nitrate above the extreme impurity level are localities categorized by a hefty amount of agricultural activities [6].

Geographic Information System can be used to measure the nitrogen content. The methodology sums up all the points and nonpoint origins of nitrogen and the data of the land area, transformations of nitrogen in the soil, and the ambiguity related to crucial soil and terrestrial passage associated variables, which help to forecast, the nitrate mass leaching to spring water. The analysis showed a total of 21 distinct terrestrial combinations was detected. The classification was done based on the several components observed from the nitrogen springs. The constituents were like fertilizers, dairy compost, and lagoons. The determinants also covered sewerage garbage like a dry and wet trash [7].

The water of purest qualities is or will become an unusual commodity in many localities and parts of the world. Food production and processing have the highest requirement of hefty loads of water of fluctuating superiority. Water can be reutilized during food production and processing and will possibly increase in the future time. From the past few years, Wastewater been used in some locations for food production. From the advent of digitization in the world, the consciousness of the nearby link between water and foodborne illness is budding. Therefore there is a requirement to improve logical water usage controlling strategies within the food production and processing business that will increase health protection in return [8].

In the Canadian part of the Abbotsford/Sumas Aquifer that has a space cover of 100 square kilometers, the three-dimensional and time-based difference of nitrate pollution was evaluated, within an experimental range. Increased nitrate levels were witnessed, over a widespread part of the aquifer of Abbotsford. A mere slight decrement in nitrate values was observed, with up to 20 m deep below the water table of earth. The outcomes came reliable with a widespread-range, non-point origin of adulteration. The three-dimensional scattering of high nitrate concentrations seemed to be associated with the terrestrial use configurations for agricultural purposes [9].

The data provided with the sensors is used to know whether there is a need to mix the chemicals to treat the water or not. By keeping an eye on the requirement, physical features of the location and needs of people, the data from the sensor can be cross-verified [10].

There is an appliance working, on a method. The content is measured by evaluating the sonic velocity in an oil-water mixture. Then to calculate the flow volume, the oil and water rates, are integrated individually. The apparatus provides an uninterrupted reading of oil and water data by determining the bi-directional velocity of sound through the moving medium with consequent frequency difference processing to derive sonic velocity, flow rate measurement, and subsequent integral data.

The present design contemplates a technique and machinery for determining content data, related to a flowing oil-water system. The invention employs a special pipe section which utilizes a mixer and straightening vane in series for providing fluid to a sonic flowmeter pipe section wherein flowmeter data, about sonic velocity and ultrasonic frequency differentials, is utilized to determine not only flow rate and volume but the percentage cut of each of oil and water within the flowing system. By using these techniques, we continually receive the percentage share of oil and water in the flow, as well as the time-integrated rates that provide uninterrupted oil and water volume data [11]. Kurokawa proposed mixing time can be more easily calculated rather than the rate of flow of liquids. He proposed an empirical method to calculate the circulation flow rate. However, mixing time measurements are time-consuming and costly. Joining time measurements also have the problem of melt contamination with the tracer material. Numerical calculations are an alternative method to overcome experimental limitations. fluid flow and concentration variations were calculated using the numerical simulations. Previous statistical studies did not estimate the circulation flow rate but calculated the deviation in concentration or the decarburization rate with assumed values for the circulation flow rates [12].

Water-consuming processes are typically modeled as either of fixed flowrate operations or fixed contaminant load operations. A new method for targeting the minimum freshwater and pinch in a single-contaminant water network is proposed, which can be applied to both kinds of operations. The method consists of plotting separate source and demand composites with flowrate as the horizontal axis and contaminant load unusually as the vertical axis. It is elegant, non-iterative, and can handle hybrid problems where both kinds of operations coexist [13].

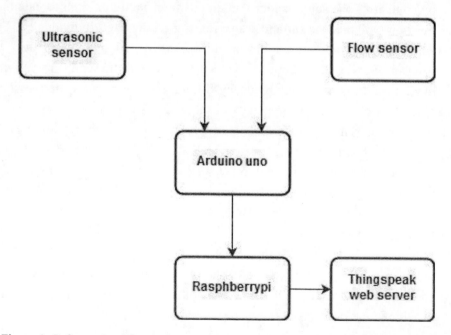

Figure 1. Software Implementation.

Software Development

The values obtained from sensors are uploaded to the Thing Speak web server. The data is analyzed, and decisions are taken, according to the data results obtained.

Hardware Description

There are various hardware used in this project. The description of all those is given in the following section of the paper:

1. Raspberry Pi
2. Arduino Uno
3. Ultrasonic Sensor
4. Flow sensor

The descriptive information about each sensor is given in the following section:

1. Raspberry PiIt is the low cost, credit card-sized computer that is plugged with the display or with some sensors. It can be attached to the keyboard or mouse of its own, which makes it eligible for the program and is used as a controller for various applications and is programmed for those applications using its operating system, for example, like in Linux in Scratch or Python. It is a kind of cheapest computer that can be programmed in various programming languages and can be used to control electronic components for physical computing and exploration of the Internet of Things (IoT).
2. Arduino Uno: It is a standard credit card-sized controller that can behave similar to the raspberry pi, but it does not own it's Bluetooth and Wi-Fi module inbuilt. It also has less memory and less accuracy of data. The Arduino Uno rev3 is a microcontroller that has dual-

inline-packaging (DIP). ATmega328 is an AVR based microcontroller. It is having 14 digital I/O pins (input/output) pins, in which 6 of them can act as PWM output, and 6 of them can act as analog inputs.

3. Ultrasonic Sensor: The ultrasonic sensor has two major components, one of them behaves as transmitter and another one act as the receiver. The transmitter first sends the eight sonic pulses of 40Khz each. It works on the principle of reflection of sound waves after striking the medium. The ultrasonic sensor is also known as HC-SR04, uses sound navigation and ranging method to calculate distance. A pulse of high (5V) for a minimum of 10us, initiates the sensing. The element will transmit eight cycles of non-audible bursts of 40kHz and expect the mirrored ultrasonic burst. When the device detects burst on the receiver, it'll set the Echo pin to high (5V) and delay for an amount (width) that proportion to distance.

4. Flow Sensor: Based on the quantification of the flow of water or bulk fluid, the flow sensor operates. It senses the flow of liquid and the rate of change of it, and thus it displays some values after measurement on the screen. The method to calculate the flow rate can be variable it can be either any of the possible ways, for example, mechanical movement or the force or torque generated on the wings of the device.

HARDWARE DEVELOPMENT

Sensors are connected to the Raspberry Pi to obtain the values like water flow rate and depth of water level. LCD is also interfaced with the Raspberry Pi to display the readings of the sensors. The Wi-Fi module will send the values to the webserver.

Power supply powers the components used. Water flow sensors and ultrasonic sensors are connected to the Arduino on port 9, A1, A0, 2, and 8th pins respectively. Raspberry Pi is connected to the Arduino by USB cable. We will use PyFirmata firmware to provide commands to Arduino using

Raspberry Pi python script. PyFirmata is primarily a prebuilt library package of python program which can be installed in Arduino to allow serial communication between a python script on any computer and an Arduino.

BLOCK DIAGRAM

Figure 3 shows the block diagram of the system to monitor the flow and depth of water. The method includes a Flow sensor, ultrasonic sensor, raspberry pi, and the power supply. The ultrasonic sensor measures the level of water, and the flow sensor evaluates the water Flow rate. The recorded values are uploaded to the ThingSpeak web server over the internet. The power supply provides power for the proper functioning of the device.

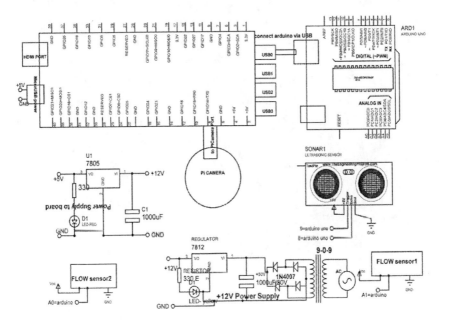

Figure 2. Circuit diagram of system.

The web server displays the values sent by sensors. The local persons can log in to the ThingSpeak web server and could look upon the values of the sensor that are found in a particular locality or part of the reservoir.

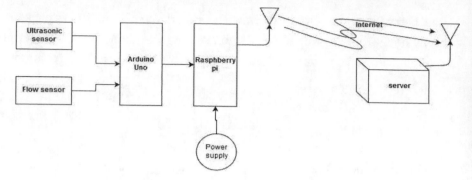

Figure 3. Block diagram of System.

RESULTS AND OUTCOME

Water level and flow rate of water are obtained and displayed on the LCD screen. The same results get simultaneously uploaded in the cloud server. The values that are obtained compared with the permissible level of impurities recommended by WHO (World Health Organization). The results which get displayed, are provided to various agencies that look after the person's life to pave the way to live easier. The data can also be useful for the authorities like NDRF (National Disaster Response Force), which can see that is there any chances of flood in the region or not and if there are chances the relief response team can work accordingly so this can also be the boon for the society.

CONCLUSION AND FUTURE SCOPE

Water quality is better managed because we get a precise measurement of impurities presents quickly by using sensors. These can be widely installed in areas where the floods are frequent. These insights enable the government to make better decisions to provide quality water to citizens.

This can be more helpful where the environment or working conditions are toxic. This can prove useful where the deployment of the human being is not worth it or dangerous. At places with such danger, to determine flow or movement with this device can act as the boon for the society.

REFERENCES

[1]   Enoki, Hideo et al. "*Water quality management system*". U.S. Patent No. 6,245,224. 12 Jun. 2001.

[2]   Chetia, Mridul et al. "Groundwater arsenic contamination in Brahmaputra river basin: a water quality assessment in Golaghat (Assam), India". *Environmental monitoring and assessment,* 173.1 - 4 (2011): 371 - 385.

[3]   Huang, Gordon, H. and Jun Xia. "Barriers to sustainable water-quality management." *Journal of Environmental Management,* 61.1 (2001): 1 - 23.

[4]   Shahanas, K. Mohammed and P. Bagavathi Sivakumar. "Framework for a smart water management system in the context of smart city initiatives in India". *Procedia Computer Science,* 92 (2016): 142 - 147.

[5]   Almasri, Mohammad N. and Jagath J. Kaluarachchi. "Modular neural networks to predict the nitrate distribution in ground water using the on-ground nitrogen loading and recharge data". *Environmental Modelling and Software,* 20.7 (2005): 851 - 871.

[6]   Lagu, Sonali S. and Sanjay B. Deshmukh. "Raspberry Pi for automation of water treatment plant". *Advances in Computing, Communications and Informatics (ICACCI, 2014 International Conference on.* IEEE, 2014.

[7]   Almasri, Mohammad N. and Jagath J. Kaluarachchi. "Assessment and management of long-term nitrate pollution of ground water in agriculture-dominated watersheds". *Journal of Hydrology,* 295.1 - 4 (2004): 225 - 245.

[8]   Almasri, Mohammad N. and Jagath J. Kaluarachchi. "IMPLICATIONS OF ON-GROUND NITROGEN LOADING AND SOIL TRANSFORMATIONS ON GROUND WATER QUALITY

MANAGEMENT 1". *JAWRA Journal of the American Water Resources Association,* 40.1 (2004): 165 - 186.

[9]   Kirby, Roy M., Jamie Bartram and Richard Carr. "Water in food production and processing: quantity and quality concerns". *Food control,* 14.5 (2003): 283 - 299.

[10] Zebarth, B. J. et al. "Agricultural land use practices and nitrate contamination in the Abbotsford Aquifer, British Columbia, Canada". *Agriculture, ecosystems and environment,* 69.2 (1998): 99 - 112.

[11] Submitter, ICAESMT Conference and Bajpai, Rishi and Singh, Rajesh and Gehlot, Anita and Singh, Pravin and Patel, Praveen, Water management, reminding individual and analysis of water quality using IOT and big data analysis (March 14, 2019).

[12] Alexander, J. D. and Reed, P. W., ConocoPhillips Holding Co, 1978. *Sonic measurement of flow rate and water content of oil-water streams.* U.S. Patent 4,080,837.

[13] Park, Y. G., Doo, W. C., Yi, K. W. and An, S. B. 2000. Numerical calculation of circulation flow rate in the degassing Rheinstahl-Heraeus process. *ISIJ international,* 40(8), pp.749 - 755.

[14] Prakash, Ravi and Uday V. Shenoy. "Targeting and design of water networks for fixed flowrate and fixed contaminant load operations". *Chemical Engineering Science,* 60, no. 1 (2005): 255 - 268.

[15] Kazemi, H., Merrill, Jr., L. S., Porterfield, K. L. and Zeman, P. R. (1976). Numerical simulation of water-oil flow in naturally fractured reservoirs. *Society of Petroleum Engineers Journal,* 16(06), 317 - 326.

In: LoRA and IoT Networks …   ISBN: 978-1-53617-164-8
Editors: A. Gehlot, R. Singh et al.   © 2020 Nova Science Publishers, Inc.

Chapter 9

THE IMPORTANCE OF INTERNET OF THINGS (IOT): APPLICATIONS AND SECURITY CHALLENGES

Rakesh Kumar Saini[1,] and Mohit Kumar Saini[2,†]*

[1]Department of Computer Science and Applications,
DIT University, Dehradun, Uttrakhand, India
[2]Department of Computer Science, Doon Business School,
Dehradun, Uttrakhand, India

ABSTRACT

The Internet of Things (IoT) revolutionized the global network comprising of people, smart devices, intelligent objects, information, and data. It is no secret that as more and more devices connect to the internet, the challenges of securing the data that they transmit and the communications that they initiate are becoming more profound. Over the years, we have seen a surge in IoT devices, broadly in 2 areas – in homes and in manufacturing. With the former, we have seen an entire ecosystem

---

[*] Corresponding Author's Email: rakeshcool2008@gmail.com.
[†] Corresponding Author's Email: mohit_kunwarpal@yahoo.co.in.

built around Amazon's Echo devices using the Alexa Voice Service. Google, Microsoft, and Apple have followed suit as well. Since these are independent and closed platforms, the responsibilities of securing the devices rest with the platform providers. In this chapter, we will discuss cybersecurity in manufacturing and related industries. Industries such as manufacturing, oil & gas, refining, pharmaceuticals, food & beverage, water treatment, and many more are constantly looking to add the right layers of security, as they bring an increasing number of equipment and devices online. Device manufacturers and plant operations managers constantly face pressure to protect their physical assets from cyber threats. Moreover, for each of these industries, the nature of the data, topologies of IoT devices, and complexities of threat management and ensuring compliance vary widely.

Keywords: Internet of Things, cyber-attack, security threats

1. INTRODUCTION

The recent rapid development of the Internet of Things (IoT) and its ability to offer different types of services have made it the fastest growing technology, with huge impact on social life and business environments. Internet of Things (IoT) devices are rapidly becoming ubiquitous while IoT services are becoming pervasive. Their success has not gone unnoticed and the number of threats and attacks against IoT devices and services are on the increase as well.

The Internet of Things (IoT) is an idea that could radically alter our relationship with technology. The promise of a world in which all of the electronic devices around us are part of a single, interconnected network was once a thing of science fiction. But IoT has not only entered the world of nonfiction; it's taking the world by storm. IoT devices are no longer a niche market. They have started to move from our workspaces into our (smart) homes, where IoT devices are expected to have the most significant impact on our daily lives. Most smart home devices will be benign, everyday appliances like kettles and toasters. Even if these devices are hacked and compromised, short of ruining your breakfast, there's not a lot a hacker can do to cause you grief. The market is currently focusing on the vertical domains of IoT since it is in relatively early phases of development. But IoT cannot be treated as a single thing, or single platform, or even a single technology. In order to achieve the expected rapid growth from IoT opportunities, more focus needs to be put on interfaces, platforms, mobile applications and common/dominant standards [1, 2].

IoT in the education sector has already started to make the conventional education system more automated — interactive smart classrooms are helping students learn and participate more, whilst automatic attendance and various student tracking systems could help to make schools more secure. Internet-enabled remote classrooms will be a milestone for developing countries, making deep penetration in areas where setting up a traditional school infrastructure is not possible. Internet-enabled manufacturing and industrial units are giving differentiating results, making them safer and more efficient through automated process controls. Plant and energy optimization, health and safety control and security management are now increasingly being provided by advanced sensors, networked with sophisticated microcomputers. Financial services are already leveraging the internet for many of their services. Exponential improvement in digital infrastructure and the next generation of IoTenabled products could further lead the growth of the financial sector, with innovations, such as smart wearable and smart monitoring devices, helping customers to keep better track of their money and investments. Telcos could face a surge in data usage due to IoT-enabled devices, thus raising their ARPU (average revenue per user), while on the other hand, they will also have to deal with some concerns, such as privacy and infrastructure security. While the possibilities of these new technologies are mind-boggling, they also reveal severe IoT cybersecurity challenges. During the last few years, we've seen a dramatic increase in the number and the sophistication of attacks targeting IoT devices. The interconnectivity of people, devices and organizations in today's digital world, opens up a whole new playing field of vulnerabilities — access points where the cyber criminals can get in. The overall risk "landscape" of the organization is only a part of a potentially contradictory and opaque universe of actual and potential threats that all too often come from completely unexpected and unforeseen threat actors, which can have an escalating effect. In this chapter discussed various security challenges in IOT. This chapter presents an analysis of recent research in IoT security from 2016 to 2019, its trends and open issues. The main contribution of this chapter is to provide an overview of the current state of IoT security challenges [3].

2. INTERNET OF THINGS (IOT)

The internet of things, or IoT, is a system of interrelated computing devices, mechanical and digital machines, objects, animals or people that are provided with unique identifiers (UIDs) and the ability to transfer data over a network without requiring human-to-human or human-to-computer interaction A thing in the internet of things can be a person with a heart monitor implant, a farm animal with a biochip transponder, an automobile that has built-in sensors to alert the driver when tire pressure is low or any other natural or man-made object that can be assigned an IP address and is able to transfer data over a network [4, 5].

Increasingly, organizations in a variety of industries are using IoT to operate more efficiently, better understand customers to deliver enhanced customer service, improve decision-making and increase the value of the business. The internet of things (IoT) is a computing concept that describes the idea of everyday physical objects being connected to the internet and being able to identify themselves to other devices. The term is closely identified with RFID as the method of communication, although it also may include other sensor technologies, wireless technologies or QR codes [6].

The IoT is significant because an object that can represent itself digitally becomes something greater than the object by itself. No longer does the object relate just to its user, but it is now connected to surrounding objects and database data. When many objects act in unison, they are known as having "ambient intelligence." Internet of Things (IoT) is an ecosystem of connected physical objects that are accessible through the internet. The 'thing' in IoT could be a person with a heart monitor or an automobile with built-in-sensors, i.e., objects that have been assigned an IP address and have the ability to collect and transfer data over a network without manual assistance or intervention. The embedded technology in the objects helps them to interact with internal states or the external environment, which in turn affects the decisions taken [7].

3. CHARACTERISTICS OF INTERNET OF THINGS (IOT)

You can define the Internet of Things by looking at the various characteristics in the broader context. We see all of these characteristics coming back in most Internet of Things definitions out there (further below is an overview with some of these IoT definitions).

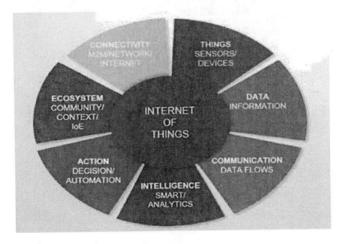

Figure 1. Characteristics of Internet of Things.

3.1. Intelligence

IoT comes with the combination of algorithms and computation, software & hardware that makes it smart. Ambient intelligence in IoT enhances its capabilities which facilitate the things to respond in an intelligent way to a particular situation and supports them in carrying out specific tasks. In spite of all the popularity of smart technologies, intelligence in IoT is only concerned as means of interaction between devices, while user and device interaction is achieved by standard input methods and graphical user interface [8].

Together algorithms and compute (i.e., software & hardware) provide the "intelligent spark" that makes a product experience smart. Consider Misfit Shine, a fitness tracker, compared to Nest's intelligent thermostat. The Shine experience distributes compute tasks between a smartphone and the cloud. The Nest thermostat has more compute horsepower for the AI that make them smart.

3.2. Connectivity

Connectivity empowers Internet of Things by bringing together everyday objects. Connectivity of these objects is pivotal because simple object level interactions contribute towards collective intelligence in IoT network. It enables network accessibility and compatibility in the things. With this connectivity, new market opportunities for Internet of things can be created by the networking of smart things and applications. Connectivity in the IoT is more than slapping on a WiFi module and calling it a day. Connectivity enables network accessibility and compatibility. Accessibility is getting on a network while compatibility provides the common ability to consume and produce data. If this sounds familiar, that's because it is Metcalfe's Law and it rings true for IoT [9].

3.3. Dynamic Nature

The primary activity of Internet of Things is to collect data from its environment, this is achieved with the dynamic changes that take place around the devices. The state of these devices change dynamically, example sleeping and waking up, connected and/or disconnected as well as the context of devices including temperature, location and speed. In addition to the state of the device, the number of devices also changes dynamically with a person, place and time. The state of devices change dynamically, e.g., sleeping and waking up, connected and/or disconnected as well as the context of devices including location and speed. Moreover, the number of devices can change dynamically.

3.4. Enormous Scale

The number of devices that need to be managed and that communicate with each other will be much larger than the devices connected to the current Internet. The management of data generated from these devices and their interpretation for application purposes becomes more critical. Gartner (2015) confirms the enormous scale of IoT in the estimated report where it stated that 5.5 million new things will get connected every day and 6.4 billion connected things will be in use worldwide in 2016, which is up by 30 percent from 2015. The report also forecasts that the number of connected devices will reach 20.8 billion by 2020 [10, 11].

The number of devices that need to be managed and that communicate with each other will be at least an order of magnitude larger than the devices connected to the current Internet. Even more critical will be the management of the data generated and their interpretation for application purposes. This relates to semantics of data, as well as efficient data handling.

3.5. Sensing

IoT wouldn't be possible without sensors which will detect or measure any changes in the environment to generate data that can report on their status or even interact with the environment. Sensing technologies provide the means to create capabilities that reflect a true awareness of the physical world and the people in it. The sensing information is simply the analogue input from the physical world, but it can provide the rich understanding of our complex world.

We tend to take for granted our senses and ability to understand the physical world and people around us. Sensing technologies provide us with the means to create experiences that reflect a true awareness of the physical world and the people in it. This is simply the analog input from the physical world, but it can provide rich understanding of our complex world [11, 13].

3.6. Heterogeneity

Heterogeneity in Internet of Things as one of the key characteristics. Devices in IoT are based on different hardware platforms and networks and can interact with other devices or service platforms through different networks. IoT architecture should support direct network connectivity between heterogeneous networks [12]. The key design requirements for heterogeneous things and their environments in IoT are scalabilities, modularity, extensibility and interoperability. The devices in the IoT are heterogeneous as based on different hardware platforms and networks.

They can interact with other devices or service platforms through different networks.

3.7. Security

IoT devices are naturally vulnerable to security threats. As we gain efficiencies, novel experiences, and other benefits from the IoT, it would be a mistake to forget about security concerns associated with it. There is a high level of transparency and privacy issues with IoT. It is important to secure the endpoints, the networks, and the data that is transferred across all of it means creating a security paradigm.

There are a wide variety of technologies that are associated with Internet of Things that facilitate in its successful functioning. IoT technologies possess the above-mentioned characteristics which create value and support human activities; they further enhance the capabilities of the IoT network by mutual cooperation and becoming the part of the total system [12, 13].

As we gain efficiencies, novel experiences, and other benefits from the IoT, we must not forget about safety. As both the creators and recipients of the IoT, we must design for safety. This includes the safety of our personal data and the safety of our physical well-being. Securing the endpoints, the networks, and the data moving across all of it means creating a security paradigm that will scale [14].

4. APPLICATIONS OF INTERNET OF THINGS (IoT)

IoT has many applications, but today we will cover top 11 IoT Applications with uses. So, let's explore them one by one.

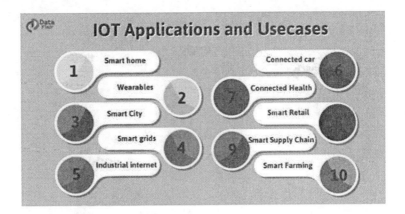

Figure 2. Applications of Internet of Things.

4.1. Connected Health (Digital Health/Tele Health/Telemedicine)

IoT has various applications in healthcare, which are from remote monitoring equipment to advance & smart sensors to equipment integration. It has the potential to improve how physicians deliver care and also keep patients safe and healthy. Healthcare IoT can allow patients to spend more time interacting with their doctors by which it can boost patient engagement and satisfaction. From personal fitness sensors to surgical robots, IoT in healthcare brings new tools updated with the latest technology in the ecosystem that helps in developing better healthcare. IoT helps in revolutionizing healthcare and provides pocket-friendly solutions for the patient and healthcare professional [15, 16].

Connected healthcare yet remains the sleeping giant of the Internet of Things applications. The concept of connected healthcare system and smart medical devices bears enormous potential not just for companies, but also for the well-being of people in general. Research shows IoT in healthcare will be massive in coming years. IoT in healthcare is aimed at empowering people to live healthier life by wearing connected devices. The collected data will help in personalized analysis of an individual's health and provide tailor made strategies to combat illness. The video below explains how IoT can revolutionize treatment and medical help [17, 18].

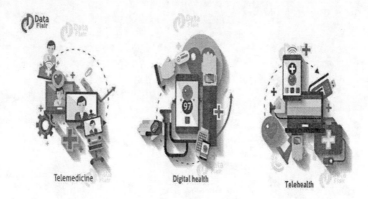

Figure 3. Connected Health.

4.2. Smart City

Smart city is another powerful application of IoT generating curiosity among world's population. Smart surveillance, smarter energy management systems, automated transportation, water distribution, urban security and environmental monitoring all are examples of internet of things applications for smart cities. IoT will solve major problems faced by the people living in cities like pollution, traffic congestion and shortage of energy supplies etc.

Products like cellular communication enabled Smart Belly trash will send alerts to municipal services when a bin needs to be emptied [19].

Figure 4. Smart City.

By installing sensors and using web applications, citizens can find free available parking slots across the city. Also, the sensors can detect meter tampering issues, general malfunctions and any installation issues in the electricity system.

4.3. Connected Cars

The automotive digital technology has focused on optimizing vehicles internal functions. But now, this attention is growing towards enhancing the in-car experience. A connected car is a vehicle which is able to optimize its own operation, maintenance as well as comfort of passengers using onboard sensors and internet connectivity. Most large auto makers as well as some brave startups are working on connected car solutions. Major brands like Tesla, BMW, Apple, Google are working on bringing the next revolution in automobiles [20, 21].

Connected car technology is a vast and an extensive network of multiple sensors, antennas, embedded software, and technologies that assist in communication to navigate in our complex world. It has the responsibility of making decisions with consistency, accuracy, and speed. It also has to be reliable. These requirements will become even more critical when humans give up entirely the control of the steering wheel and brakes to the autonomous or automated vehicles that are being successfully tested on our highways right now.

Figure 5. Connected Cars.

4.4. Smart Home

Smart Home has become the revolutionary ladder of success in the residential spaces and it is predicted Smart homes will become as common as smartphones Whenever we think of IoT systems, the most important and efficient application that stands out every time is Smart Home ranking as highest IOT application on all channels. The estimated amount of funding for Smart Home startups exceeds $2.5 bn and is ever growing. Wouldn't you love if you could switch on air conditioning before reaching home or switch off lights even after you have left home? Or unlock the doors to friends for temporary access even when you are not at home. Don't be surprised with IoT taking shape companies are building products to make your life simpler and convenient [22].

The cost of owning a house is the biggest expense in a homeowner's life. Smart Home products are promised to save time, energy and money. With Smart home companies like Nest, Ecobee, Ring and August, to name a few, will become household brands and are planning to deliver a never seen before experience.

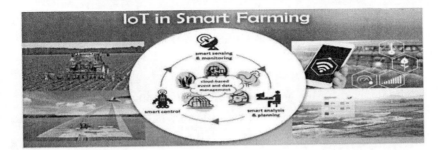

Figure 6. Smart Home.

4.5. Smart Farming

Smart farming is an often overlooked IoT application. However, because the number of farming operations is usually remote and the large number of livestock that farmers work on, all of this can be monitored by the Internet of Things and can also revolutionize the way farmers work. But this idea is yet to reach a large-scale attention. Nevertheless, it still remains to be one of the IoT applications that should not be underestimated. Smart farming has the potential to become an important application field specifically in the agricultural-product exporting countries [19].

Figure 7. Smart Farming.

4.6. Smart Retail

Retailers have started adopting IoT solutions and using IoT embedded systems across a number of applications that improve store operations such as increasing purchases, reducing theft, enabling inventory management, and enhancing the consumer's shopping experience. Through IoT physical retailers can compete against online challengers more strongly. They can regain their lost market share and attract consumers into the store, thus making it easier for them to buy more while saving money.

The potential of IoT in the retail sector is enormous. IoT provides an opportunity to retailers to connect with the customers to enhance the in-store experience. Smartphones will be the way for retailers to remain connected with their consumers even out of store. Interacting through Smartphones and using Beacon technology can help retailers serve their consumers better. They can also track consumer's path through a store and improve store layout and place premium products in high traffic areas [24].

4.7. Smart Supply Chain

Supply chains have already been getting smarter for a couple of years. Offering solutions to problems like tracking of goods while they are on the road or in transit, or helping suppliers exchange inventory information are some of the popular offerings. With an IoT enabled system, factory equipment that contains embedded sensors communicate data about different parameters such as pressure, temperature, and utilization of the machine. The IoT system can also process workflow and change equipment settings to optimize performance.

Figure 8. Smart Supply Chain.

5. INTERNET OF THINGS (IoT) SECURITY

IoT security is the protection of Internet of Things devices from attack. While many business owners are aware that they need to protect computers and phones with antivirus, the security risks related to IoT devices are less well known and their protection is too often neglected.

Internet of Things devices are everywhere. From cars and fridges to monitoring devices on assembly lines, objects around us are increasingly being connected to the internet. The speed at which the IoT market is growing is staggering Juniper research estimates that the number of IoT sensors and devices is set to exceed 50 billion by 2022. While consumer IoT devices allow lifestyle benefits, businesses are quickly adopting IoT devices due to high potential for savings. For example, after Harley-Davidson turned their York, Pennsylvania plant to a 'smart factory' using IoT devices in every step of the production process, they reduced costs by 7% and increased net margin by 19% [22].

5.1. Security Challenges Facing IoT

5.1.1. Data Integrity
Billions of devices come under the umbrella of an interlinked ecosystem that is connected through IoT. Manipulating even a single data point will result in manipulation of the entire data which is exchanged and shared back and forth from the sensor to the main server. Decentralized distributed ledger and digital signatures should be implemented in order to ensure integrity.

5.1.2. Encryption Capabilities
Data encryption and decryption is a continuous process. The IoT network's sensors still lack the capability to process.

The brute force attempts can be prevented by firewalls and segregating the devices into separate networks.

5.1.3. Privacy Issues

IoT is all about the exchange of data among various platforms, devices, and consumers. The smart devices gather data for a number of reasons, like, improving efficiency and experience, decision making, providing better service, etc.; thus, the end point of data shall be completely secured and safeguarded [23].

5.1.4. Common Framework

There is an absence of a common framework and so all the manufacturers have to manage the security and retain the privacy on their own. Once a common standardized framework is implemented, the individual efforts will then collectively be utilized in an expandable manner and so reusability of code can be achieved.

Figure 9. Security Challenges Facing IoT.

5.1.5. Automation

Eventually, enterprises will have to deal with more and more number of IoT devices. This enormous amount of user data can be difficult to manage. The fact cannot be denied that it requires a single error or trespassing a single algorithm to bring down the entire infrastructure of the data.

5.1.6. Updations

Managing the update of millions of devices needs to be adhered to, respectively. Not all the devices support over the air update and hence it requires manually updating the devices. One will need to keep a track of the available updates and apply the same to all the varied devices. This process becomes time-consuming and complicated and if any mistake happens in the process than this shall lead to loopholes in the security later. Security Investment in securing infrastructure and network should be the first priority, which is not the case now. IoT involves the use of millions of data points and each point should be secured. Indeed, the need is for the multi-layer security, i.e., security at each and every level. From end-point devices, cloud platforms, embedded software to web and mobile applications that leverage IoT (Internet of Things), each layer should be security intact. With the set of heterogeneous devices, security becomes complex [24].

5.2. How to Maintain IoT Security

While securing your endpoints and network will depend on what types of devices you have, there are certain precautions that will help you to secure any type of IoT gadget or appliance.

5.2.1. Use Strong Passwords

Having strong passwords is always important, but especially so for IoT devices. With a weak password, taking control of an IoT device through its own interface or web portal is trivial. What's even more concerning is that many IoT devices come with default passwords, which many users don't change – meaning that the attacker may already know the password to your device?

Strong passwords on the rest of your network will also add a second line of defence if an attacker does gain access through a device – stopping or hindering their attempts to access files, databases, and other devices. Changing the password on your router to a long and strong one is especially important, as a compromised router quickly leaves the whole network vulnerable.

5.2.2. Network Security

Ensure that you have an up-to-date, secure router, with a firewall enabled. Your router can be the first point of attack– and if your router is compromised it will leave your entire network vulnerable. Installing an endpoint security solution that allows you to discover vulnerabilities in your network – for example, one with a scan feature such as Avast's Wi-Fi Inspector - is essential.

5.2.3. Patches

Responsible manufacturers will release security updates for their IoT devices when vulnerabilities are discovered. Ensuring your devices are patched regularly with the latest updates is important. If you have a device that doesn't receive updates, consider the benefits of the device against the potential impact on your business in the event of an attack.

5.2.4. Consider Necessity

As there is a growing market for IoT devices, manufacturers are eager to pump out large numbers of them, and may not spend much time developing their product's security. While IoT devices can be highly useful, consider whether your office kitchen really needs that internet-enabled toaster or kettle. While the benefits of new technology always seem exciting – especially for small business owners looking to save money and increase productivity – it's important to take time to understand the risks that come with it. IoT devices have the potential to bring efficiency improvements to many industries, but steps should also be taken to ensure they don't leave your network vulnerable to malicious actors.

6. IoT Identity Protections

Cyberspace and real life are merging. With the Internet of Things (IoT), individuals and devices are increasingly connected to the Internet and physical objects are continuously integrated into information networks. Machines and robots are able to sense and analyze data, enabling control of the physical world. The IoT will bring about many major changes. But these big changes make way for new challenges, particularly with respect to security. The stored data contains highly detailed information about an individual, and that gives a clear picture of the individual-that includes details about our financial circumstances, our health, our religious preferences, and our family and friends; giving the criminals all the information they need to take advantage of someone. People may also not be aware of the level of privacy; for example, entertainment devices may gather audio and video data, and share intimate information. When the IoT systems fail or malfunction, they can cause substantial damage; private data may get leaked the smart phones that we carry everywhere with us are connected to a no. of devices. We take them to busy places, public places and use them naturally in front of strangers, for any purpose. It's not hard for someone to watch someone type in their device's pin code or password and it's all easy to memorize a security code and steal the device. If the thief is using your Smartphone and your device's data and act as you on your behalf and impersonates the identify which may lead to the loss of much bigger things-General data available on the internet, combined with social media information, plus data from smart watches, fitness trackers and if available smart meters, smart fridges and many more give a great all-round idea of your identity. Any time that you establish an account with a username, password, and other identifiable information, you're leaving that digital trail about you. Identity theft can therefore be counted as one of the biggest risks in the IoT. Security is essential for IoT, especially with respect to identity. Therefore, security should be designed into IoT systems from the beginning, not tacked on later [23].

6.1. IoT-Identity Protection

Identity of an individual must be protected in IoT; it is must to confidentially hold the personal details of any consumer.

Various steps need to be taken to secure identity theft in IoT. Some of them are:

1. Have strong and unique passwords
2. Do not over share personal information
3. Safeguarding your information, whether it's related to your credit card or your thermostat, should be a constant priority.
4. For connectivity via Wi-Fi, it is better to use a VPN like PRIVATE Wi-Fi for mobile devices connecting to.IOT devices.
5. It is always wise to share as little information as possible when using services, and never select "remember my details" such as for personal banking or corporate networks.
6. Ensure that your data is encrypted and only authorized people have access to the data
7. .Smartphone for proper authentication on IoT devices.
8. Multi-factor authentication requires a combination of objects to gain access – usually two or more of something you know (e.g., a password), something you have (e.g., your phone) and something you are (e.g., a fingerprint). This improves your security.
9. Use a different password for every device and always change the default password.•
10. Give IoT sensors and devices their own digital identities. You can do this by converting select bits of information about each one into a digital record.
11. Cryptographic authentication is the best approach to IoT device identity. IoT devices are fully capable of establishing, maintaining, and employing long cryptographic keys. There is no reason to employ passwords for device identity.
12. Installing smart chips in each sensor.
13. Monitor the systems and devices periodically.
14. Ensure IoT users awareness; make the users know what details to share, how to keep their password strong and secured.

Figure 10. IoT-Identity Protection.

CONCLUSION

The IoT framework is vulnerable to attacks at each layer. Therefore, there are many security threats and requirements that need to be dispatched. Current state of research in IoT is mainly concentrated on authentication and access control protocols, but with the rapid growth of technology it is essential to consolidate new networking protocols like IPv6 and 5G to achieve the progressive mash up of IoT topology The main emphasis of this chapter was to highlight major security issues of IoT particularly, focusing the security attacks and their countermeasures. Due to lack of security mechanism in IoT devices, many IoT devices become soft targets and even this is not in the victim's knowledge of being infected. In this chapter, the security requirements are discussed such as confidentiality, integrity, and authentication, etc. In this survey, twelve different types of attacks are categorized as low-level attacks, medium-level attacks, high-level attacks, and extremely high-level attacks along with their nature/behavior as well as suggested solutions to encounter these attacks are discussed. We hope this chapter will be useful to researchers in the security field by helping identify the major issues in IoT security and providing better understanding of the threats and their attributes originating from various intruders like organizations and intelligence agencies.

REFERENCES

[1] R. Vignesh and 2A. Samydurai ans1 Student, 2Associate Professor Security on Internet of Things (IOT) with Challenges and Countermeasures in 2017 IJEDR | Volume 5, Issue 1 | ISSN: 2321-9939.

[2] N. Koblitz, "Elliptic curve cryptosystems," *Mathematics of computation,* vol. 48, 203-209, 1987.

[3] J. Y. Lee, W. C. Lin, and Y. H. Huang, "A lightweight authentication protocol for internet of things," in *Int'l Symposium on Next-Generation Electronics* (ISNE), 1-2, 2014.

[4] Y. Xie and D. Wang, "An Item-Level Access Control Framework for Inter-System Security in the Internet of Things," in *Applied Mechanics and Materials*, 1430-1432, 2014.

[5] B. Anggorojati, P. N. Mahalle, N. R. Prasad, and R. Prasad, "Capability-based access control delegation model on the federated IoT network," in Int'l Symposium on Wireless Personal Multimedia Communications (WPMC), 604-608, 2012.

[6] M. Castrucci, A. Neri, F. Caldeira, J. Aubert, D. Khadraoui, M. Aubigny, et al., "Design and implementation of a mediationsystem enabling secure communication among Critical Infrastructures," *Int'l Journal of Critical Infrastructure Protection*, vol. 5,86-97, 2012.

[7] R. Neisse, G. Steri, and G. Baldini, "Enforcement of security policy rules for the internet of things," in *Int'l Conference on Wireless and Mobile Computing, Networking and Communications* (WiMob), 165-172, 2014.

[8] Mirza Abdur Razzaq and Muhammad Ali Qureshi "Security Issues in the Internet of Things (IoT): A Comprehensive Study" by (IJACSA) *International Journal of Advanced Computer Science and Applications*, vol. 8, No. 6, 2017.

[9] J. S. Kumar and D. R. Patel, "A survey on internet of things: Security and privacy issues," *International Journal of Computer Applications*, vol. 90, no. 11, 2014.

[10] M. Abomhara and G. M. Køien, "Security and privacy in the internet of things: Current status and open issues," in Privacy and Security in Mobile Systems (PRISMS), *International Conference* on. IEEE, 2014, pp. 1–8.

[11] S. Chen, H. Xu, D. Liu, B. Hu, and H. Wang, "A vision of iot: Applications, challenges, and opportunities with china perspective,"*IEEE Internet of Things journal*, vol. 1, no. 4, pp. 349–359, 2014.

[12] L. Atzori, A. Iera, and G. Morabito, "The internet of things: A survey," *Comput. Netw.*, vol. 54, no. 15, pp. 2787–2805, Oct 2010.

[13] M. M. Hossain, M. Fotouhi, and R. Hasan, "Towards an analysis of security issues, challenges, and open problems in the internet of things," in Services (SERVICES), 2015 *IEEE World Congress on. IEEE*, 2015, pp. 21–28.

[14] L. Da Xu, W. He, and S. Li, "Internet of things in industries: A survey,"*IEEE Transactions on industrial informatics*, vol. 10, no. 4, pp. 2233–2243, 2014.

[15] L. M. R. Tarouco, L. M. Bertholdo, L. Z. Granville, L. M. R. Arbiza, F. Carbone, M. Marotta, and J. J. C. de Santanna, "Internet of things in healthcare: Interoperatibility and security issues," in Communications (ICC), *IEEE International Conference on. IEEE*, 2012, pp. 6121–6125.

[16] Mohan, "Cyber security for personal medical devices internet of things," in Distributed Computing in Sensor Systems (DCOSS), 2014 *IEEE International Conference on. IEEE*, 2014, pp. 372–374.

[17] Mohamed Abomhara and Geir M. Køien" Cyber Security and the Internet of Things: Vulnerabilities, Threats, Intruders and Attacks".

[18] S. De, P. Barnaghi, M. Bauer, and S. Meissner, "Service modelling for the internet of things," in Computer Science and Information Systems (FedCSIS), 2011 *Federated Conference on. IEEE*, 2011, pp. 949–955.

[19] G. Xiao, J. Guo, L. Xu, and Z. Gong, "*User interoperability with heterogeneous iot devices through transformation*," 2014.

[20] J. Gubbi, R. Buyya, S. Marusic, and M. Palaniswami, "Internet of things (iot): A vision, architectural elements, and future

directions,"*Future Generation Computer Systems*, vol. 29, no. 7, pp. 1645–1660, 2013.

[21] M. Zorzi, A. Gluhak, S. Lange, and A. Bassi, "From today's intranet of things to a future internet of things: a wireless-and mobility-related view," *Wireless Communications, IEEE*, vol. 17, no. 6, pp. 44–51, 2010.

[22] C. Hongsong, F. Zhongchuan, and Z. Dongyan, "Security and trust research in m2m system," in Vehicular Electronics and Safety (ICVES), 2011 *IEEE International Conference on. IEEE*, 2011, pp. 286–290.

[23] Cha, Y. Shah, A. U. Schmidt, A. Leicher, and M. V. Meyerstein, "Trust in m2 communication," *Vehicular Technology Magazine, IEEE*, vol. 4,no. 3, pp. 69–75, 2009.

[24] Lopez, R. Roman, and C. Alcaraz, "*Analysis of security threats, requirements, technologies and standards in wireless sensor networks.*"

In: LoRA and IoT Networks ...   ISBN: 978-1-53617-164-8
Editors: A. Gehlot, R. Singh et al.   © 2020 Nova Science Publishers, Inc.

Chapter 10

IOT IN FIRE SAFETY-AN EXCITING FUTURE FOR SMART BUILDING AND CITIES

Gajanand S. Birajdar[1,], Rajesh Singh[2†]
and Anita Gehlot[2‡]*
[1]SRCOE Pune, SPPU, Maharashtra, India
[2]Lovely Professional University, Jalandhar, Punjab, India

ABSTRACT

A smart city is an objective of the Indian government which is meant to provide cities with infrastructure and give a decent quality of life to its citizens, clean and sustainable energy sources. It uses the internet of things to collect data and uses these data for managing assets and resources efficiently. With the rapid growth in the construction industry, buildings are becoming smart with the deployment of smart things. Smart Cities and Buildings need to inherently be Safe and secure. Most of our upcoming cities have high rises and dense concentration of buildings, making it even more essential to rapidly and effectively address any type of fire situation

---

[*]Corresponding Author's Email: gajananbirajdar20@gmail.com.; Gajanand S Birajdar, Assistant Professor.
[†] Corresponding Author's Email: rajesh.23402@lpu.co.in.; Rajesh Singh, Professor.
[‡] Corresponding Author's Email: anita.23401@lpu.co.in.; Anita Gehlot, Associate Professor.

to minimize and contain any loss of life and property. This chapter addresses the importance of fire safety in smart city and building along with the role of IoT in meeting the requirement.

Keywords: Smart city, Fire safety, IoT, smart building, Building Monitoring, Industry 4.0 etc

1. INTRODUCTION

The evaluation of Information and Communications technology (ICT) has enabled smarter infrastructures and cities [1]. With the addition of Internet of things to infrastructure and building, they are becoming smart enough to address problems like solid and waste management, clean and sustainable energy sources, building monitoring and many more. Sensors and actuators are main elements of IoT based smart project. Combing these elements allows owners of offices or building to save energy, increase security, give information about the environmental condition during emergency events like fire accidents [2], [4]. To support smart city vision, IoT design added value services to citizens and administration of the city. To make emergency response real-time, IoT enhances the way of response to managers [3]. The system which can address the issues like smart surveillance, Automatic Street light, weather monitoring, pollution monitoring, monitoring and alerting emergency situation like fire accidents [5]. The speed of local response and the degree of preparedness is especially important when you consider the fact that most cities have dense traffic conditions and it is unlikely that in every situation the Fire Department and its equipment reach the required locations immediately or in a timely manner. Some of the recent fire mishaps in states of India have further underlined the fact that this is not an area to be taken lightly as the consequences can be devastating. Fortunately, there are emerging technologies which can be leveraged to enhance the effectiveness and speed of the fire response. It is critical that the deployment of these should be systematized and standardized, and should go hand in hand with the evolution of our cities into smart cities that are made up of high-rises and urban sprawls.

2. EMERGING TECHNOLOGIES AS ENABLERS

The confluence of a few emerging technologies offers us new options to enable a step-change in how safety can be addressed in our upcoming Smart buildings and smart cities. To be truly considered 'Smart' these buildings and cities should be able to rapidly and more coherently address emergency situations if such an event occurs. Also, they must equally focus on those elements that can help prevent the occurrence of such fire situations. Some of the key technologies that could enable such a change include

- *The explosive growth and easy access to internet connectivity & bandwidth* Internet is the vehicle for communication of data both large and small. It allows almost instant communication of information in both a 'push' and 'pull mode'. Given the strides in wireless technologies like 4G, LTE and in Fiber technologies, both internet and bandwidth are economical and accessible in most places urban and rural. This is the backbone of the Internet of Things (IoT) technologies being discussed here.
- *The ubiquity of Smart Phones and Tablets* along with their inbuilt notification systems Devices that can access the internet must be present ubiquitously in the hands of users to provide them with the right information at the right time. Smartphones, tablets, etc., have become economical and rapidly increasing in adoption making this the vehicle of choice for enabling Fire Safety. Android and iOS-based notifications have added to the traditional voice, email and SMS based systems thereby providing redundancies in communication to users, which are very essential in emergencies.
- *Advancement of wireless technologies*, especially for IoT enabled sensors Quick and reliable detection of the fire event occurrence is critical to enable fire safety. Sensors have always been the

mechanism to do that in many western countries. The latest advances though have allowed these sensors to communicate wirelessly using RF to reach the internet and communicate events instantaneously. Long battery lives and communication of their battery status and their functional health is now feasible for these devices, which make them even more easy to maintain and more importantly, also to be more fail-safe.

- *Economical access to Cloud-based Apps and data storage* A large network of sensors and users does require correspondingly sized applications and data storage capabilities. The emergence of multiple 'cloud' service providers makes this an economical option that can be used for things that range from monitoring the health of sensors to serving data and notifications to first responders and other users.

- *Adoption of Computer-aided Facility Management (CAFM), Building Information Modeling (BIM) and virtual reality (VR) technologies* for efficient operation and management of buildings Accurate data about buildings, such as the floor layout, building assets, fire-fighting equipment, evacuation plans and also its occupants is critical for the First Responders and Emergency Crew on the scene. CAFM, BIM, and VR are some of the emerging technologies that store and serve this data for various uses that range from the daily operation of facility management to emergency response situations.

3. AN IOT BASED SYSTEM FOR FIRE SAFETY

These emerging technologies when aligned together to complement each other, can deliver the promise of enhanced Fire Safety, enabling the promise of Smart buildings and cities that are safer.

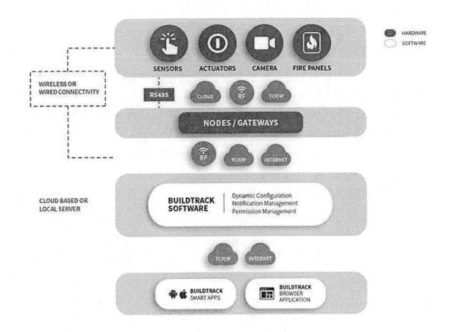

Figure 1. IoT system architecture.

A typical architecture of such an IoT system is shown in Figure 1. At the edge of the system sit the pieces of hardware that actually detect the fire. Typically these are constituted by Fire Panel systems or sensors of some kind, usually Smoke, Gas Leak, Temperature or similar other. The next level of the system consists of hardware that communicates with the prior layer either via wired means such as shielded RS485 or CAT6 cabling or through some form of wireless RF signals. This layer typically consists of hardware called as Nodes, Hubs or Gateways. Typically these Nodes, Gateways or Hubs are pieces of hardware which have access to the Internet either through wired or wireless means. This layer communicates with the Cloud application server using IP protocol and communicates any event that is sensed by the 'edge' devices such as fire panels or sensors that are connected with it. The health of the system is being checked by each layer on an ongoing basis and communicated to the cloud server. This health monitoring activity is as critical as the monitoring of any fire event itself, because the usefulness of the whole setup is dependent on the system being in a 'healthy' state. So not only are the events themselves important, but other aspects such as battery levels of the sensor or panels, the RF connectivity between the sensors and the Gateway/Nodes and the internet availability at the Gateway/Nodes. The cloud server is the repository of all the event and health information and it also houses information pertaining to the actual real estate in which the sensors and panels are housed. Such information can consist of Floor plans, Fire Evacuation plans, Building Asset information, Fire Fighting Equipment information, Fire Audit Information, Occupant Information and where applicable even surveillance cameras. All this critical information needs to be linked to specific sensor information so that if a fire event occurs, not only are the first responders and affected occupants being made aware of the event, but also accompanying relevant and actionable information that will result in saving of life and property.

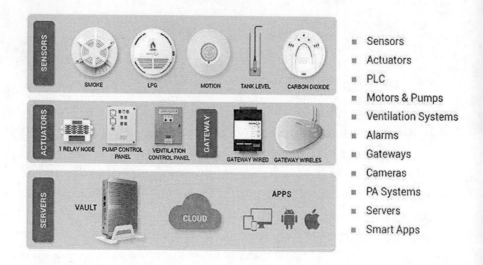

Figure 2. Fire monitoring and control elements in the system.

In addition, the Cloud Server application supports notification management, i.e., the automated and manual ability to communicate with all occupants connected with the affected property areas to guide them through the event. This communication can occur through App notifications, emails, SMS and PA systems. These communication tools can be engaged by the administrators of the application based on how the emergency situation or event evolves.

The first responders and occupants can use Smart Apps or Browser-based applications or hard kiosks to access the Cloud Server and the information that it provides. Absent any of the above, they can still access SMS messages or PA system that the application would send out thereby allowing broad coverage to ensure that almost all do receive the relevant information.

There are a number of other aspects that this architecture can enable, besides just sensors and fire panels. Figure 2 shows some of these elements that the system can link together. These elements can relate to;

a. Verification: Cameras, Motion Sensors, and other such devices can serve as useful tools for verification of fire or movement of people in a specific area. The same system can be connected to allow an integrated view of all these aspects that are critical to the first responders in arranging the fire-fighting and rescue efforts

b. Status and Control of Assets: Pumps, Motors, Elevators, Ventilation Systems etc which are all building assets whose status is important to be known in the event of a fire. These can be connected to the same system to provide firefighters with an integrated view of some critical assets as it relates to the fire.

Figure 3. Centralized fire monitoring platform.

The system when deployed has the ability to serve needs at various levels – Individuals, Building Operators and Centralized Fire Safety Departments that extend across geographies. Information can either be aggregated or segregated at any level geographically for monitoring sensor information. Figure 3 shows an example of such a centralized monitoring setup that is monitoring a broad geography for occurrence of emergency events. The system can also serve as a mechanism to escalate emergency events if need be.

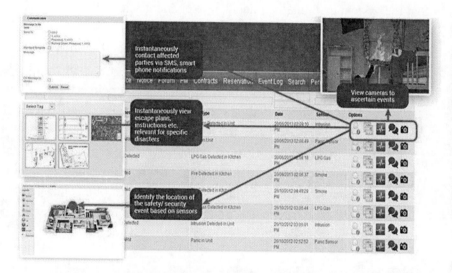

Figure 4. Platform enables a variety of actions in the event of an emergency.

One of the principal benefits of such a platform is that can be used by organizations to efficiently and effectively addresses emergencies. Figure 4 shows an example of how as emergency events occur and are communicated by a sensor to the system, a menu of actions can be provided to the people who respond. This menu of actions can support the following

a. Understanding the location of the fire event in the context of floor plans or building layouts

b. Verification of the fire event, by opening up linked cameras to verify the ground conditions

c. Communication via email, notifications, SMS and PA systems to occupants of affected areas

d. Understanding the various options by looking at the fire escape plans and/or other information

These are examples only, and other such actions that facilitate rapid and effective responses can all be enabled for the firefighters and other responders. An additional and important facet addressed by such systems is to maintain relevant property, asset and occupant information along with fire inspection and audit information for the property all of which may be critically needed not only while addressing a fire situation but also to ensure that buildings are in compliance with fire regulations on an ongoing basis thereby reducing the likelihood of such fire-related emergencies. An example of such data that might be available is displayed in Figure 5.

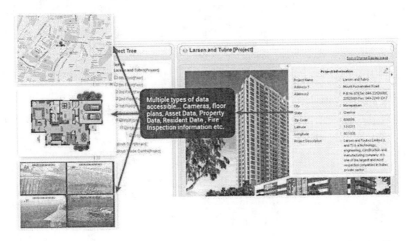

Figure 5. Platform stores all relevant information on Property, Assets, Fire Audits and more.

CONCLUSION

An Internet of Things (IoT) enabled sensing technology with the accompanying gateways that connect to backbone cloud-based software and apps is a critical requirement for upcoming Smart cities, buildings, and neighborhoods to enable fire safety. Such an IoT based system can significantly improve the speed and effectiveness of the response, within any geography big or small, by providing relevant and actionable information about IoT System Architecture the event, the property and the occupants to the first responders and those caught in the fire event. Such a system also plays a pivotal role in ensuring compliance with fire audits and inspections so that occurrences of such emergency events themselves are hopefully minimized by an escalation of non-compliance. This system, therefore, is fundamental in making Smart cities into safer cities.

REFERENCES

[1]   Giorgio Cavalera, Roberto Conte Rosito, Vincenzo Lacasa, Marina Mongiello, Francesco Nocera[3], Luigi Patrono[4], and Ilaria Sergi, *"An Innovative Smart System based on IoT Technologies for Fire and Danger Situations,"* 2019 4th International Conference on Smart and Sustainable Technologies (SpliTech), DOI: 10.23919/SpliTech.2019.8783059, IEEE-2019.

[2]   Nicolas Havard, Sean McGrath, Colin Flanagan, Ciaran MacNamee, *"Smart Building Based on Internet of Things Technology",* 2018 Twelfth International Conference on Sensing Technology (ICST), DOI: 10.1109/ICSensT.2018.8603575, IEEE- 2018.

[3]   Ravi Kishore Kodali, Subbachary Yerroju, *"IoT Based Smart Emergency Response System for Fire Hazards",* 2017 3rd International Conference on Applied and Theoretical Computing and Communication Technology (iCATccT), DOI: 10.1109/ICATCCT.2017.8389132, IEEE-2018.

[4]   Timothy Malche, Priti Maheshwary *"Internet of Things (IoT) for*

building Smart Home System", 2017 International Conference on I-SMAC (IoT in Social, Mobile, Analytics and Cloud) (I-SMAC), DOI: 10.1109/I-SMAC.2017.8058258, IEEE-2017.

[5] Dr. Madhvi A. Pradhan, Supriya Patankar, Akshay Shinde, Virendra Shivarkar "IoT for Smart City: Improvising Smart Environment", International Conference on Energy, Communication, Data Analytics and Soft Computing (ICECDS-2017), DOI: 10.1109/ICECDS.2017.8 389800, IEEE-2017.

[6] S.R.Vijayalakshmi, S.Muruganand, *"Internet of Things technology for fire monitoring system,"* International Research Journal of Engineering and Technology (IRJET), Volume: 04 Issue: 06, June - 2017.

EDITOR'S CONTACT INFORMATION

Anita Gehlot

Lovely Professional University, Jalandhar, Punjab, India
eranita5@gmail.com

Rajesh Singh

Lovely Professional University, Jalandhar, Punjab, India

Ravindra Kumar Sharma

Department of Electronics and Communication Engineering,
Ambedkar Institute of Advanced Communication Technologies

Kamal Kumar Sharma

Lovely Professional University, Jalandhar, Punjab, India

INDEX